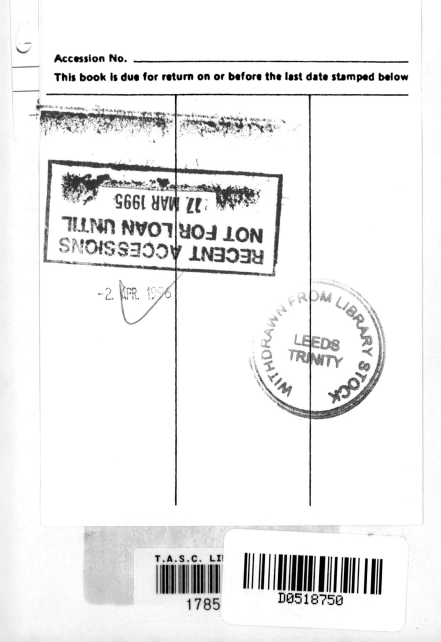

The Thousand and One Mornings

ALSO BY COLETTE

Colette

The Thousand and One Mornings

Translated from the French by
MARGARET CROSLAND AND DAVID LE VAY

and with an Introduction by
MARGARET CROSLAND

PETER OWEN · LONDON

ISBN 0 7206 0441 9

Translated from the French
Contes des mille et un matins

PETER OWEN LIMITED
12 Kendrick Mews Kendrick Place London SW7

First British Commonwealth edition 1973
© 1970 Flammarion, Paris
English translation © 1973 Peter Owen

Printed in Great Britain by
A. Wheaton & Co Exeter

Contents

Introduction

In the *Tales of 1001 Mornings* Colette appears not as a twentieth century Scheherazade but as an imaginative and energetic journalist; this book contains some of the articles she contributed to the French daily newspaper *Le Matin* on the eve of the first world war. After her divorce from her first husband, 'Willy', early in the century, Colette had appeared on the Paris stage as a mime and travelled all over France with a theatrical touring company, while at the same time she had continued to publish one book a year. She wrote once that the music-hall was the profession of those without a profession, and although she also said the same of journalism, it lay nearer to her vocation as a writer.

She joined *Le Matin* in 1910 when the paper was co-edited by Henri de Jouvenel, later to become her second husband. From 1919 to 1922 Colette took over the literary editorship of this enterprising newspaper which had been founded in the late nineteenth century by Alfred Edwards. When she first contributed to it Colette was a courageous reporter at a period when the profession was still dominated by men. Old photographs show her dressed for risky aeroplane flights or riding in the basket of the airship *Clément-Bayard*. She made the most of her varied subjects, enjoying any opportunity to write about the theatre or the absurdities of fashion. She always enjoyed watching the behaviour of women, analysing their appearance, attitudes and motives. She was quick to criticize them if they took themselves too seriously and equally quick to praise them when they asserted their fragile independence or courageously accepted the hard, underpaid work which women in France could hardly avoid at this period.

At the same time she observed with a novelist's eye leading political figures and dangerous criminals, with the result that the

11

reader can see and hear them, the former in the Chamber of Deputies, the latter in the courtroom. Many of the articles here are memorable for the feeling of rapid movement they convey, whether they describe a manhunt or the Tour de France. Colette's technique varies from the oblique description to the dramatic monologue and includes some amusing examples of the 'one-sided dialogue', a method she developed with success and used on other occasions.

The range of the articles is wide and gives a clear impression of the people and events which interested and amused the readers of *Le Matin* between 1911 and 1914. Most of these articles remained unpublished in book form in France until 1970 but Colette's publishers believed that the reports of this 'exceptional observer' should not be forgotten, especially since the years on which she was reporting 'contained, beneath a deceptive appearance of frivolity, many germs of our future troubles'. These 'tales' also include a short volume first published in 1918 under the title *Dans la foule.*

Some of the articles have short introductory pieces giving the background. I am indebted to Rayner Heppenstall for details about the Bonnot gang and the background to 'A Dinner on 17 March'.

M.C.

Conquest of the Air

The Bubble

A bubble which rises into the air, round, well-inflated, golden-coloured, encased within its netting: our balloon. The little car that bears us away seems a tiresome accessory, serving only to delay and deface this beautiful globular-type balloon whose departure has the slight hesitation and uncontrollable caprice of some bird's wing, but a wing rebellious to the will of man and capable of trifling with him.

It rises quickly and we think it slow. Its imaginary slowness is reassuring, and almost disappointing, for the aeroplane and the motor-car have led to an automatic association between a rush of air and the notion of speed. The wind, which previously held the tethered balloon flat against the ground and rocked the trees in the park, the wind now consists of us, the five of us. Apart from the pilot the car contains the inexperienced but intrepid passenger, the famous lawyer, the seasoned lady traveller, and me. The sides of the car carry, I am assured, enough wine, sandwiches and chocolate to make a landing in deserted country as pleasant as a garden-party.

A bag of ballast empties out into the Seine as we cross it and penetrates the water with the delightful sound of beads falling. As for us, we are smiling, we are confident, astonished only at moving along without the deafening assistance of an engine, without leaving behind us a trail of smoke, or the smell of petrol, oil or heated iron. . . .

'Six hundred . . . only seven hundred and fifty feet. . . . My friends, please listen a moment! We're leaving the Eiffel Tower on our left, aren't we?'

'Yes, yes, old man, we are . . .'

The pilot is the only spoil-sport at this departure. His devoted sagacity restricts our irresponsible delight, and what have we in common with the Eiffel Tower? Instead of remaining satisfied and contemplative like us, why must this pilot fiddle with useless instruments and obstinately pinch the rubber tubing which hangs

15

down from the round belly of the statoscope? We very nearly reward his zeal by commiseration and insults, urging him not to get agitated. . . . Our golden-coloured bubble goes up and up. . . . Why can't he be calm in the same way? . . .

'We're going past the Tower, aren't we?'

'Yes, yes, old man, we are . . .'

This pilot's wonderful! If you listened to what he says you'd think that the Eiffel Tower blocked every route through the air, and that we don't know whether we'll find beside it a little corridor of wind to take us over there, towards that beautiful misty south-east. . . .

The pilot, who's more patient than any man has the right to be, makes no reply. . . . Perhaps he's regretting he took dangerous lunatics up with him. . . . And since he busies himself with measuring out careful little spadefuls of the ballast which protects us from the Tower, he lets himself be treated in a friendly way as a 'grocer'.

'Fifteen hundred . . . two thousand, four hundred . . . three thousand feet. . . . My friends, don't be frightened by the jerk. I'm going to undo the guide-rope.'

. . . Three hundred feet of cable are hanging down from the car at the moment, and beneath the free end of the cable there is still . . . brrr . . . there is still over half a mile of empty space. For a moment the demon of dizziness, swinging on the quivering end of the guide-rope, beckons to me. . . . But it's a passing weakness and I soon forget it as I recognize the suburbs of Paris, its multi-coloured surface, its zinc roofs, its squares and clumps of trees, its bald spots and its blemishes . . . three thousand, six hundred feet. . . . Paris moves away beneath trails of purple smoke, to which the Sacré-Coeur, through a ray of sunshine, brings a harsh, dramatic light. A storm, which is rolled up in a corner of the sky, seems to go down as we go up. The beauty of the sky and the earth, simplified and magnified by our ascent, calms us. Terrestrial sounds no longer reach the cool air where we are hovering, and we remain silent for a long time, until one of us says half aloud, in spite of himself : 'This silence . . .'

. . . Paris is lost, down there, far away already. A glinting patch indicates every bend in the Seine; gardens enclosed by walls reveal to us the secrets of their châteaux protected by forests, the orderly clarity, the unaffected carpet of their French-style gardens. . . .

'Four thousand, five hundred feet . . .'

The clean, dry air, tasting of snow, brings on the urge to eat and drink; the approaching dusk also revives in us a possibly anxious solidarity and respect – at last! – for the irreproachable pilot. The seasoned lady traveller gives him a glass of sparkling wine, the inexperienced but intrepid passenger offers the assistance of his long arms, while the famous lawyer promises the pilot an invincible plea in his defence, 'just in case, and it could happen, you're involved in some sordid matter . . .'

The pilot smiles gently, like a patient Newfoundland dog tormented by playful puppies. He leaves us to our pleasure, alternately grave and gay; he gives us all he can of the birdless, cloudless sky, the flat world where the distant forests are blue, where towns throw out their suburbs round about them like divergent beams of a star; he looks at the lozenge-patterned shadow of the rope-net immediately beneath the protruding stomach of our golden bubble before saying, 'My friends, we shall have to land', before throwing out the opened newspaper which goes down, hovers motionless, then suddenly twists in frenzy, wheels round like a wounded seagull and falls. . . .

Buzzing in our ears, near-enjoyable deafness, we're going down. . . . A velvety forest becomes singularly clear, how is it that I can suddenly make out its russet and green trees, and its round-headed giants? The sound of a waterfall comes up to us, along with a scent just as cool, slightly bitter: the scent of oak-trees after rain. . . . What a surge of bird-calls seems to celebrate our return to earth!

'Get down, everyone! Cover your heads and hands!' the pilot's voice calls out.

We've just had time to obey when the car, which had come down on to the forest, scrapes the tops of the trees with the crash of broken twigs and torn leaves. Above us the flabby sides of the balloon, which has now gone thin, shudder and struggle. . . . A gust of wind takes us up again and carries us away; I hear a musical twang as we cut through the telegraph-wires and I stand up to watch two splendid, plump, mud-coloured huntsmen running below us, hanging from the guide-rope as it drags along, so out of breath and so comical. . . . We soon outdistance them and I become quite tense as I see rushing towards us two venerable walnut-trees, planted at the top of a sloping field. They won't give way like mere telegraph-wires. . . . But the pilot is there! With a rough and masterly hand he saves our lives by pulling the ripcord: a bump, and the car, like an overturned basket, empties us out on to the dry grass of a mown field, all in a heap with the statoscope, the barometer, the last bags of ballast, the bottles of wine, the peaches and, alas, the chocolate creams. . . .

Little to fear, and no harm done. The centre of interest is the limp-lying balloon, the beautiful bubble that is now burst, killed by each barbarous landing, still quivering as, with each heaving breath, a little more of its dying strength ebbs away.

Up There

Ever since the early 1850s important achievements in airship design were made in France, notably the experiments of the Brazilian Santos-Dumont at the turn of the century. For ten years or so before the First World War the French government airship factory and design centre and at least three other firms constructed lighter-than-air, non-rigid or 'pressure' airships like the one described here. They embodied an internal ballonnet which could be pumped up with air to preserve the shape of the envelope without loss of gas. The non-rigid airship *Clément-Bayard* had been built by the company of the same name at La Motte-Breuil, near Compiègne.

13 June, 1912

What's the matter with them? How they're shouting, suddenly. They're shouting cheerfully, they're waving their hands and throwing their heads back! It's the change in their attitude, and then the way they grow smaller, closer together and disappear, that makes me realize we're going up. The *Clément-Bayard* has just left the ground; no jolt, no shuddering warned me of it. In the same way the ripe seed detaches itself from the calyx of the thistle, rising imperceptibly, and begins to float without our guessing at what moment it ceases to be held. . . .

They're melting away, melting away beneath us. Their shouts reach us in shrill scattered fashion. . . . A little while ago this was a dense crowd, getting in our way and preventing the airship from coming out. Now they mark the square like a handful of black shot. . . .

So it's really true then, we're going up! This iron balcony, this carriage without any seats that I compared, in the hangar, to a tram in summer; this steel floor, this bridge made entirely of resonant heavy metal, this baggage piled up in the narrow end of the car; and the group of officer instructors and my companions and I, we're all going up serenely, hanging from the airship's silken belly, hanging from the yellow balloon like a new-hatched chick! I insist on gazing with dulled eyes at the little black crowd just below us. . . . I can't believe . . . But the roaring of the engines which so far had been silent, the fresh breeze from the propellers, awaken in me the reassuring sensation of movement, effort, travel, and I turn round avidly in order to see Paris coming towards us! . . .

Then I give way suddenly to utter delight, expressed in astonished 'oh's' and ecstatic 'ah's', a cheerfulness which is in fact almost incomprehensible : is the fact of travelling at six hundred feet above Paris enough to explain it? . . . Delight it is, however, unclouded, ageless joy, a foolish joy consisting of leaning very hard against the railing in order to discover with astonishment that there is 'nothing holding us underneath'! A different joy from that which I relished during a short flight in a biplane, for the active, noisy and skilful take-off, the élan of the aeroplane banish the feeling of disturbance from which I am now emerging, the anxiety during which I was able to wonder for an instant if I was dreaming or if, miraculously, I was rising towards the sun like a bubble. . . .

Paris unfurls beneath us. It has been photographed so often

from the sky that I recognize it easily, the complicated network of its streets, its star-shaped squares, its rivers and islands form a plan which is already familiar. It is these details of colour and contour that I like, roofs that are strangely blue or angry and red; the lakes in the public parks glitter and go out, a train begins to curl round like an irritated caterpillar. . . . It is the compactness of the town that delights me, the fact of finding it almost small and untidy. . . . Its stifling confusion only stops in respectful fashion to leave a little air round the handsome edifices : the Louvre and its clear-cut gardens are restful to the eye, the outline of the Luxembourg can be read like a clear picture. Abundant young trees in regular rows make each cemetery into an attractive enclosure. . . .

But through what wretched gaps among the modern close-set houses do the laden air and miserly light come down? How shapeless our houses are, how close to the colour of dirty butter, beside the old buildings which are delicately, eternally grey. The old quarters are the most beautiful, those which time, soot, worn stone and coal-laden rain have covered with a subtly-coloured ash. I lean down, regretting that we must pass them so quickly, over the last few gardens, shut off in the depths of black buildings, unsuspected by passers-by, languishing and adorned like valuable captives. . . . During the first moments, did I not fly over one of these flowerbeds, the one where an acacia flowered, near a long strip of grass, the one where a glass-roof glitters? . . . I didn't think of it in time. . . . The idea that I have – down there where the Seine glitters and curves – a place of shelter which includes everything I love, touches me for a moment but without warmth and without force. My pleasure, which is too new and too potent, forgets in inhuman fashion *those down there*. . . .

I can still see those down there. They're black, as nimble as working insects, sometimes motionless, suddenly in groups : when they stop we know that they're looking at us. Our incredible journey which makes men stand stock-still, scatters the dogs; black, yellow or white, their forms can be seen running in all directions and hiding. . . .

But . . . Is that the end of Paris already? Tiny little Paris, crossed in a few minutes ! . . . We're going up, we're turning. . . . The airship's slender tail describes a gentle arc over the horizon made smoky by the town : the country with its market gardens, green and squared, appears. Flat, flower-filled and inhabited, it possesses hardly any other beauty than its riches, this false tatter-demalion patched with velvet of a hundred different colours. We look right down into the vertical stalks of wheat, right into the light barley, as into the deep pile of a shadowy plush. . . . Here and there, toy-like villas enclose their acre of land, their trees and flowers, surrounded with new walls, reminding us of the small-scale boundaries traced by children with white pebbles or shells round a sand castle. . . .

As we go higher, everything on earth acquires an extreme pre-cision, becoming smaller still and simplified. 'Oh look', I shout, 'they've combed that field so carefully. . . . And why have they built such a twisting road there? . . .' Since taking off I've been talking about them as though I would never go down to earth again. There are two races : those below and ourselves, we who pass by in the sky. In the car are two or three travellers who are also making their first ascent; I see they are like me, curious and detached from what is going on down below, strangers too to the idea of crashing or danger, or even dizziness, conditioned from the first moment to the miracle of flight. In order to impose it on the people below, we invent a new architecture, a decorative coquetry which they should display for us. . . .

A grasping sense of security stems from our delight; we ask the master of this fine ship for endless journeys, for soothing nights at three thousand feet, awakenings in the clouds, for twilights like this one, red and striped with black, where there is still enough sunshine to touch the church spires in one, two or ten scattered villages. . . .

'It's getting dark', one of us says. We didn't think of it as long as the sunset glow remained, while the panorama of villages, gleaming rivers and forked roads was still clear. But now we're going along above a dark outline, a forest of dull green which absorbs the failing light. . . . It is the forest of Compiègne, spread out like magnificent curly fabric. Man is biting into it, alas ! At its edges can be seen the teeth-marks of mice and deep breaches, and round holes, which show up its exposed weft.

The forest of Compiègne ! The end of the trip. . . . I'm neither the only one nor the first to sigh : 'What a pity !' . . . Our regrets are so fervent you might think we were not coming down but crashing into an ungrateful hillside. . . .

With the tranquil infallibility of a pigeon returning to its nest the airship moves towards its hangar of bluish iron visible in the middle of a field. The meadows, the elder-hedges grow bigger, come up towards us. Cables are already falling from the car into the midst of a group of soldiers who haul us down without a jolt. . . . We are the prey of men without wings. . . .

Up there, in the June sky, still pale from the prolonged daylight, nothing marks our passage through the air. It's dark. My feet sink into the wilting mown grass which is all cold with dew. A shrub brushes against my hand as though it had been searching for it; a heavy late insect buzzes and hangs from my hair. . . . How strong is the scent of the elders this evening, the scent of the syringas, the freshly-mown hay, the damp mint! The nocturnal earth takes hold of us again and caresses us in the darkness; a jealous friend, betrayed for a moment, conquering us again because it smells so sweet. . . .

At the Air Show

Le Matin, 18 December, 1913

Only four years ago at Dijon, I was present at the timid departure, the hesitant flight, and finally the slow descent of an aeroplane piloted by a novice. I remember how the white bird, as it touched the ground, cracked with the dry snap of a piece of wood being broken, I remember that nothing was left of it except a little snapped-off timber, some metal, a limp, broken white wing – and fortunately the man was safe. The crowd, who were astonished and slightly disappointed, searched the scattered remains for the shape of the fine monoplane whose shadow had been so big just before over the field. . . .

Why should I remember this descent of the wounded pigeon, still supported by the air? Gleaming metal, pink copper, bluish steel, the cold grey of aluminium, the blackness of cast iron; engines shaped like heavy rose windows, cylinders, tubes, arms, hooks – metal, metal and still more metal! – everything that can inspire and nurture the idea of weight, immobility, unbending and inflexible strength is there in front of me, and all that is destined for the kingdom of the air. They fly, these ingots, these bastions, these drums, these polished shafts.

These towers and iron platforms go forward along a pathway of clouds. . . . And the white bird, the bird of flapping cloth, stripped of its wing by a puff of wind, has lived; here, selected and transformed by the merciless genius of those who reared it, is its almost unrecognizable offspring : this little impetuous monster, the squat, rigid shell, totally iron-clad, with its short boxer's nose and its body with receding sides. Seen in profile, it is expressive and alive, slightly comic like certain raging beasts. One of these, crouching on its folded paws, clings to its wheels, eyeing space with an impetuous, impatient air, and extends the thick short armature of an organ which is half-atrophied : the wing, which will soon be of no use to its meteoric speed.

News Items

While Watching Houssard Accused of Killing and Mme Guillotin Accused of Loving.

This article concerns a crime which caused much stir in 1912. Paul Houssard had murdered Guillotin by shooting him twice in the back of the neck. Houssard may have been Madame Guillotin's lover but he seems to have been particularly interested in the money which her husband had arranged to leave to her. Houssard was condemned to twenty years' penal servitude.

Henri Robert, one of the legal personalities mentioned by Colette, was one of the best assize lawyers of the day. Mademoiselle Laudereau was a friend of Madame Guillotin.

27 June, 1912

Horrible day of internment, immobility, suffocation, disappointment! A day which began in the wait for some new excitement, a day which gathered together all the scattered remnants of a fine tragedy, just as Donner, bringing the clouds together, liberated the thunderbolt! Nothing has emerged: no shout, no sob, no irrepressible confession, and the interminable day ends in boredom and somnolence.

Outside the entrance to the court the public, who were not very discreet, showed signs however of a somewhat sinister, feverish gaiety. Many women had come for *her*, motivated by a barely concealed hostility. . . .

I had expected more gravity among those present. These gentlemen of the law courts press, brimming over with joviality, blossom out into teasing forecasts. The atmosphere? . . rather that of an afternoon dress-rehearsal, and moreover here is Capus. If I mention details the theatrical impression becomes clearer: the empty platform, half-broken doors, floorboards, badly tied-up parcels, the bric-à-brac of some second-rate décor. I allow myself

27

to be so much influenced by the cynical light-heartedness of my companions that I forget these dilapidated doors have served as targets, that these roped bundles contain clothing still rigid with dried blood.

The entrance of Paul Houssard brings me back to reality. He sits down and shows only his profile. Not once will he turn round towards the public. For seven hours we shall see only his honest profile, which is ordinary, apart from the obstinate shape of his broken nose. This stubborn outline and this unbending neck remind me to a remarkable extent of Captain Meynier, the murderer of Baroness Olivier. Houssard speaks, and once again it is the voice of Captain Meynier, blurred, embarrassed and soft, and this even goes for the strange shake of the head indicating 'No' when the accused man replies 'Yes, Your Honour'.

Then begins the most interminable, the most soporific dialogue between the President Roussel and the accused. Dialogue, what am I saying? Monologue, a presidential monologue uttered with exasperating slowness; repetitions, useless digressions; insistence without penetration; a tentative preoccupation with detail that wearies all ears and discourages even the most impassioned attention! Only some cutting interruption by M. Henri Robert and a feline reply from M. Maurice Bernard interrupt this tepid stream of words from time to time, for Houssard, who is frustrated and almost incapable of speech, ravaged by nervous tics, can only reply by saying : 'I don't know, I can't remember.'

He barely murmurs, without gesticulation, and his voice rises slightly, only to affirm : 'There was nothing between Mme Guillotin and myself.'

Nothing indicates if he is upset by the very precise questions put to him on this subject. He simply utters denials. He protests against the evidence, with the limited calmness of a gallant man.

The brief and silent appearance at the hearing of Mme Guillotin, wearing her black veils, overwhelms him. The accused man seems to feel her presence like someone breathing quickly, he swallows with difficulty, as though he had swollen tonsils. He looks at her often and sharply, he leans towards her as though drawn by a magnet.

Of her, I can only see at first the poignant spectacle of a black-gloved hand, tightly clenched in front of her face, which is hidden by a white handkerchief. But during the adjournment of the hearing, while inquisitive people try rudely to approach her, I can take my time and look at her solid face, covered with the mauvish redness which rises to the cheeks of red-headed women suffering from congestion. She has the forehead of a bull, an obstinate nose, the firm mouth of someone who eats well, and the most splendid crown of blazing hair, screwed up and brought under control with great difficulty, on the point of spreading loose and leaping out, so impatient and so full of fire that the calmness of the two big, brown eyes beneath it seems to be false.

Mme Guillotin has spoken. She has ceased to be the silent statue in mourning embarrassed by her crape.

We forget the suffocating heat and the smell of the crowded court-room because she appears; she is tall and drags her veils and cashmere coat with the impatience of a woman who is accustomed to walk uncluttered and free. People showed the same half-witted curiosity as she went by. As yesterday, I hear disgusting words and appraisals typical of cattle-drovers.

She takes her place upright in the witness-box and I listen to the sound of her voice before hearing her actual words. From the first replies in this clear-cut voice, at first strangled in her throat by emotion, but rising and growing slightly nasal when the witness becomes irritated, we are rooted to the spot. Mme Guillotin faces up to every danger. Someone shouts behind me :

'Well now, her lawyer needn't worry. She can be allowed out on her own !'

When the court was adjourned, a leading lawyer summed up in one sentence Mme Guillotin's 'manner' : 'She's like Mme Steinheil, and better.'

Once again, there in front of us, black and crowned with gleaming gold, is an incarnation of feminine courage. Once again I say to myself : 'How strong women are.'

This one has to deal not only with the court but with the public, whose aversion she can feel behind her, the public's detestable hope, they want her to be guilty ! She doesn't weaken. Weeping for a moment and saying 'I'm suffering ! My situation's terrible', isn't weakening, it's a change of method.

The tone of her replies to the Public Prosecutor is that of a woman who is being treated with a lack of respect. Sometimes she disdains any attempt to be natural and her freedom of expression occasionally arouses hostile murmurs; but these murmurs come from an irritated courtroom, from over-sensitive people astonished at hearing a woman saying: 'My husband's murderer', and the 'crime', without trembling or lowering her voice.

Mme Guillotin, who is irritable and intelligent, does not always take the trouble to master her anger. She blurts out imperious cries of 'No, no'. Sometimes she stamps her foot in a way which suits her burning face, her Junoesque, slightly animal forehead. Every over-strong expression seems to adorn this colourful face where everything becomes animated as soon as she speaks : avid nostrils, cheeks softened with tears, eyebrows tending to join together.

She was a coquette, to be certain, and proud of herself, glad to inspire love. With barely concealed pleasure she repeats : 'My husband loved me passionately, he saw only me. M. Houssard felt for me an intense, a really abnormal passion.'

M. Houssard, that is how she describes carefully, without a single mistake, the man who killed on her behalf and who takes care not to admit he was her lover. He is still there, so pale, so inert, as though forgotten. But he listens when she speaks, he shudders and sits up automatically when he is questioned, then he falls back and leans tensely towards the delight of hearing at last the voice he loves. . . .

During the adjournment, which follows her deposition, Mme Guillotin rests like an athlete between rounds. Languid, relaxed, letting all her muscles go and all her strength lie dormant, she awaits the procession of witnesses. Did she fear this file-past of pale servants who had been dismissed, venomous neighbours, a sardonic and timid manservant, a young, indecisive German woman and the stammering Mlle Laudereau, all those who have poured floods of rancour into the court against Mme Guillotin and Paul Houssard, and who are now silent in the witness-box, drawing back, stammering, forgetful, retracting what they had said and going away with their heads lowered in front of everyone present?

We are embarrassed, sickened. These sordid anecdotes about

walls with holes drilled in them, curtains lifted at corners, lost hairpins, this trade union of espionage, lying, perhaps of calumny, finally revolt us. We are nearly on the point of turning back, in order to absolve him, towards that being who is both heroic and cowardly simultaneously and only opens his mouth to testify: 'She is innocent. I loved her. . . . She did not want to belong to me. . . . I killed because I loved. . . .'

In the Crowd

After the Rue Ordener Affair

The two following articles are about the notorious 'Bonnot gang'. Jules Bonnot was a mechanic from Lyon who had organized the theft of motor-cars on a large scale, in addition to other criminal activities. He was an anarchist and joined forces with over twenty other men sharing the same beliefs. The group specialized in bank raids and 'the Rue Ordener affair', which took place in Montmartre, is said to be the first recorded hold-up in the world. After this incident Bonnot and one accomplice barricaded themselves into a garage-hut at Choisy-le-Roi, south of Paris. In spite of protecting himself with mattresses, Bonnot was wounded by police bullets and finally shot himself.

The trial of the Bonnot gang lasted three weeks. Carouy and Callemin were Belgians, the latter, who was well-read, being known as 'Raymond Science'. Kilbatchiche, the 'intellectual' of the gang, was of Armenian origin and later wrote and published books under the name of 'Victor Serge'. His good-looking, intelligent girl-friend 'Rirette' Maîtrejean edited the news sheet *L'Anarchie*. Although Bonnot himself had said that Dieudonné was innocent, he was sentenced to penal

servitude for life but escaped from Guiana and was rehabili-
tated. Carouy committed suicide. Four of the accused were
sentenced to death and the others imprisoned.

2 May, 1912

There's something over there. . . . It's beyond the crowd, which
has been stopped by a barrage of policemen and Paris guards,
the crowd which spreads out in uneven streams along the sides
of the road and stagnates in long black puddles. . . . It's behind
the flinty, heavy dust which flies up like spray from waves.
There's something over there on the right of the main road,
something which everyone is looking at and nobody sees. . . .

I've just arrived. In order to push forward to the front row
I've used, in turn, the brutality of a woman customer during a
sale at a big store, and the deceitful niceness of weak creatures :
'Sir, let me go past. . . . Oh, Sir, I'm being suffocated. . . . Sir,
you're so lucky to be so tall.' . . . They've allowed me to come
through to the first row because there are hardly any women in
this crowd. I touch the blue shoulders of a policeman – one of the
pillars propping up the cordon – and I'm aiming to go still further
forward. . . .

'Officer . . .'

'No one's to go through!'

'But those people running over there, look, you're certainly
letting them go through. . . .'

'Those are the gentlemen of the press, and besides they're men.
Even if you did belong to the press, anyone wearing a skirt must
stay here quietly.'

'Would you like my trousers, Madame?' suggests a voice with
a suburban accent.

There is very loud laughter. I remain silent. I look at the road
which is sealed off by intermittent hurricanes. Like everyone else
I'm aiming at a spot which is beyond the dust and the curtain
of trees : a grey hut, and the angle of its roof which has been put
on sideways. . . . I stay where I am, a prey to the agitation of a
sightseer : 'What's going on? What have they done already?
Where are they?'

The policeman is facing the road and no longer answers me;

my neighbour, a person without a hat, sheltering a child under each arm, looks me up and down. I behave very politely:

'Tell me, Madame, are they down there, the bandits?'

'Certainly they are, Madame, in that hut on the right.'

The intonation signifies clearly: 'Where have you been? Everybody knows that!' A big quiet chap, standing just behind me, supplies me with the information:

'They're inside. So to stop them escaping again they're going to be blown up with dynamite.'

'Blown up, oh go on, I'll bet ten to one that they'll beat it and leave everyone standing.'

This sporting reply comes from a pale young man with a cynical look, who is moreover continuously active: he's leaning craftily against his neighbours and he's jostling against me with a show of clumsiness. I'll wager that at the first opportunity he's going to lower his head, push through under the policeman's arm and rush on to the empty road.

They're over there, they're going to be blown up. This disgusting spectator-spirit takes hold of me, the same spirit which takes women to bullfights, boxing-matches and even to the foot of the guillotine, the spirit of curiosity which so perfectly replaces real courage. I shift from one foot to the other, I lower my head to protect myself from the clouds of dust. . . .

'Now Madame, do you think it's easy to see anything when you're standing near to someone as fidgety as you?'

That's my severe neighbour, the mother with her children. I mutter and she goes on crudely:

'That's a fact, that is, there's no point in being here since 9 o'clock this morning just for you to put yourself in front of me at the last minute! If I've booked a place, I've booked it, and people with hats should take them off.'

She protects her 'orchestra stall' with an authority which seeks – and finds – general approval. Behind me I hear rhythmic shouts: 'Hat! Hat!' and jokes which date from last year's reviews, but here they take on a strange flavour when you think of what's going on over there. . . .

Suddenly the wind bring us, along with the dust which gets between our teeth, the obvious and startling smell of burning: over there it's no longer the dust that's sealing off the road but

the blue-grey colour of smoke blown violently about in the wind.
. . . The shouts, behind me, go up like flames :

'They're there! Can you hear? I heard it go off! The house
has been blown up. No, it's gun-fire, they're running away,
they're running away. . . .'

Nobody has seen anything or heard anything, but this nervous
crowd who are hemming me in on all sides are inventing, unconsciously, by telepathy perhaps, everything that's going on over
there. A thrusting movement which has been prepared in advance
and cannot be withstood, breaks through the cordon and carries
me forward; I run to avoid being crushed; I run at the same time
as my neighbour and her two nimble children. The sporty cynical
young man pushes me aside with a rough movement of his
shoulder, a thousand others come behind. We run, making as
much noise as a herd of animals, towards the goal which is more
invisible than ever, *over there*. . . .

A sudden stop, then a movement backwards which half knocks
me over. After falling to my knees I hang on to two strong arms
which at first shake me angrily, then they haul me along; I've no
time to say 'thank you'. 'Where are they? Where are they?' A
thin working girl in a black apron pants : 'They've escaped!
They're running across the fields! Everyone's running after them!'

She can't know, she hasn't seen anything. She shouts and
describes aloud what she imagines. The mob takes hold of the
two of us again and bears us away; I shelter for a moment against
a very tall man who allows himself to be bandied about and
pushed around in an impersonal sort of way, his two raised arms
holding a camera up in the air, operating it non-stop, just
guessing. . . .

The dust and smoke are suffocating. . . . As the wind blows
away the cloud covering us I notice that I'm very near the
battered hut which is crackling and burning; but all at once the
crowd sweeps me away and I struggle to avoid them crushing
me. . . . People are shouting in a confused way; the voices are
hoarse and muffled like those of people sobbing. Shouting becomes clear, spreads, and the tumult turns into a regulated noise :
'Kill them! Kill them!' I breathe, thanks to a gap. . . .

'Kill them! Kill them!' Again I'm pushed and bruised,

knocked against the boot of a car which is being opened, and *something*, heavy, long and inert, is hoisted into it. . . .

None of the people who are shouting near me and around me can see what's going on; but they're shouting through contagion, imitation, can I say through conventionality?

'Kill them! Kill them!'

This blond quarry worker barks mechanically, his eyes staring; a plump southerner says in an oily tone of voice 'Kill them!' just as he might say 'Of course' or perhaps 'Encore' at the café-concert. I watch in astonishment as two milliner's girls, as gay as if they were at the open-air market in Neuilly, walk along arm in arm, give way beneath the shouts, allow themselves to get free, stop calling out 'Kill them, Kill them' and burst out laughing. . . .

Between the heads, between the moving shoulders, I catch sight of the hovel enveloped in flames. . . . A man leans from a torn-out window and throws down a mattress and sheets soaked in blood so copious and so pink in the bright light of noon that it looks artificial. . . .

'Kill them!'

How excited and angry the shouts are growing! I feel the car shudder and start slowly. I must take to my heels immediately if I don't want to be trampled under the feet of those following it. . . . As it goes it seems to magnetize and drag with it the entire crowd. . . .

At last I can slow down and stop. The car and its screaming escort move away like a black storm. Already the white road on the Paris side is covered with a voluble crowd, still half unaware of what the car took away. Separated from the mass of the crowd I remain for a long moment in front of the bouquet of flames fed by dry wood, the magnificent and cheerful flames which move about in the strong wind. That's where they were hanging out. . . .

I was a remnant of the crowd, oppressed and blind, I'm becoming lucid again. I'm off in my turn to Paris, to find out what drama I've just attended. . . .

The Gang

From the place I occupy I can't see all of them. In the first row I can easily recognize Soudy, Kilbatchiche and Callemin further away, and then Dieudonné. Carouy in the second row is visible to me from time to time, placed in a blue and red frieze of municipal guards.

I recognize them, thanks to the newspapers which for so many days have been showing them to us from the front, side and back. But they seem hardly more alive to me here than they did in the snapshots and endless sketches which made their features familiar to me. It's certainly the exhaustion of twelve consecutive court appearances that makes them lifeless and sleepy, and they suffer gloomily the dreary studio light which comes from above, softened by the whirling snow. The stiffness and military bearing of the guards who stand between the accused men emphasize the slackness of certain positions; I notice shoulders which have collapsed and look empty, and necks which look crooked from the back, as with the tramps who sleep on benches in the open. A large hand, of eloquent and terrible ugliness, conceals and supports a face that looks down : that hand has aimed a gun. That index finger, broadened at the tip, has pressed without trembling – how many times? – the murderous little spring. . . . I repeat this to frighten myself, in an attempt to reconstitute the gang's sinister aura. It needs a real effort. For today Dieudonné, for example – in spite of the black hair, which is blacker on the pale forehead, the charcoal effect of the eyebrows and moustache – Dieudonné has a stiff moustache and a feeble expression. Callemin, leaning, half-lying forward, his elbows sticking out and his chin on his folded hands. Callemin, who is short-sighted, active and impudent, reveals not so much insolence as self-satisfaction. This schoolboy writer of pamphlets will only say a few insignificant words today, but it is in the expression of his face, his raised eyebrows, the disdainful expression of his mouth, that his delight in an unquestioned superiority breaks out, together with the pleasure of emphasizing his 'culture' and exercising literary irony. . . .

The poison of literature! As I read the interrogations and hear the accused men speak I cannot keep seeing them as people suffering from poisoning.

Those who are least ill, the most uncultured of them, give way to the theatrical need to astonish the jury and the public, they make contact with literature as children, illiterate people and savages do : by means of drama. The naïve members of the gang reveal a veneration for the printed word, a fanatical love of the difficult word : 'Ah, tell me more words that I don't understand!' a little milliner in love would cry to her lover, as though she were giving him her soul. . . .

I think of that cry when Gauzy, after he has been pensively scribbling, stands up and reads in a voice full of concentration : 'I will ask the witness if he doesn't think I was deceived; if he isn't certain, I repeat, in all this miserable business, that I was a victim.'

This man, who is risking his life, this man, who can be innocent, has therefore drawn up his sentence with a kind of pleasure. He has written 'miserable business' and 'I repeat' between two commas. . . . With Gauzy we are obviously very far from the feeble witticisms of Callemin, and Callemin – who experienced during the court hearings the same lack of success that a local star encounters on the boulevard – appears very inferior to Kilbatchiche. Yet all three have drunk from the same dangerous cup : they have read. . . .

When Kilbatchiche gets up and begins to speak one yields at first to the triple attraction of a pleasant voice, which is easy and soft, a vocabulary more than correct, and a head which is regularly constructed without bumps or disturbing hollows, where the jaw is not monstrous and the honest skull ends in a fine forehead full of illusions. But on hearing him first demand – without brevity – permission to ask a witness a few questions, then set out – and not concisely! – a series of questions, I come to the conclusion that he is the illest of them all. To speak with a fluid elegance which seems unconscious of effort, if not of effect; to speak with a moderation of tone which excludes neither care nor exultation; to speak, for Kilbatchiche, is a delight, worse than a weakness, almost a mania.

While he concludes a chivalrous peroration in favour of Mme Maîtrejean, Dettwiller raises towards him a terrified face in which pink albino eyes blink with admiration or sleepiness; Soudy does not even turn away his clear-cut profile where the long nose juts forward while the forehead and the chin both recede. In this way, with the help of his long smooth hair, he resembles certain Red Indian faces, in which, between the flattened cheek and the sugar-loaf skull, two very small impenetrable eyes shine brilliantly. . . .

Standing up and speaking, above the rabbit with the pink eyelids and the faded Red Indian, standing close to the shapeless Bélonie, in front of Poyer (we have all more or less seen him, he's the footman of whom people say: 'I don't remember his face') Kilbatchiche continues in his clear, soft voice, he continues to pour out poison for them. Through the darkness into which they ·all feel they are descending, a word or a phrase still charms them confusedly at moments. . . . Even in the auditorium people show a kind of deference before the rhetoric of the man whom some call 'the sinister bore' . . .

But what is he thinking, the man who hardly speaks, and dreams so sombrely with his forehead on his hand? That is Carouy, who no longer hopes for anything. Does he still believe in the solidarity of those whom we have called in romantic fashion 'The Gang'? He has not turned towards them on one single occasion today. He has asked nothing from those faces round about him, where I seek in vain for the proof of a redoubtable fraternity. Pale through incarceration like Bélonie and Dettwiller, or shaken like Callemin with a disdainful gaiety, they look like people brought together here by the accidents of murder and theft. I don't succeed in feeling between them that warmth of proselytism, that hidden, slightly insane emotion which would raise an association of crooks to the level of a phalanx of rebels. Is that what Callemin in his cynical way is dreaming of? He doesn't look fierce, he looks knowing. His flared nostrils, nose and his eye are those of a subtle dog; the last 'good dog', as the huntsmen say, of a demoralised pack, where the dogs have begun to bite each other. . . .

Shall I describe the short hair, the white collar, the spotted scarf and blouse of Mme Maîtrejean? This young woman who figures in disguise, at the height of noon, at the court hearing, has had a success to which I can add nothing. She needs nobody. Her aggressive innocence is unaware of disturbance and her clothes make the comparison possible – no actress reveals on the boards a daring equal to hers. A daring which remains that of a teacher – her lively words teach and punish, the President Couinaud knows something about that! I really believed for a moment she was going to give him five hundred lines. Because of the schoolgirl's smock people called out 'It's Claudine!', but as soon as she speaks we realize that it's 'Mademoiselle'.

Modes and Manners

The Lovely Listeners

19 March, 1914

For they listen, it's a fact. Huddled close together, leaning towards the platform like corollas towards the sunlight, they are as varied as a flowerbed of pansies, where the features of each little flower-face, painted with touches of dark velvet on a background of light, smile less, or weep better, or show more surprise, than those of the flower its neighbour.

They listen, not without effort and fatigue. Lifting the chin, lowering the eyelashes, bringing the eyebrows slightly closer – that's the listener in the orchestra stalls. Leaning on her elbow with one hand on her cheek and sweeping the auditorium with a discreet slow glance – that's the lady in the boxes or the stalls. They must also smile at the right time, laugh, nod their heads, murmur with pleasure. . . . They don't fail to do so; one of them, moreover, raises and lowers her eyelids rapidly, as though someone were telling her too rapidly things which leave her breathless. Her neighbour follows the rhythm of the phrases as though she were at a concert, nodding her head and her feathers; another one punctuates the speech with a little clip of her well-known 'knives': 'Full stop. . . . Semi-colon. . . . Exclamation mark. . . .'

The truce of silence that they impose on each other marks certain faces with a singular despair. Some of them forget place and time, and reveal that tragic seriousness, that sombre and fixed attention which belongs to the solitary woman, who looks in front of her at the wall or the mirror. . . .

Three or four, at the most, fight against the desire to sleep. The species in general is too nervous to doze off during the daytime, how many of them sleep at night? I think that many of them are glad to be sitting down, because of their tight shoes and high heels. . . .

Two women friends, informed in advance, carefully check, half-aloud, the teaching of the lecturer: 'That's so . . . why not quote the letter? He doesn't say everything. . . .' And the look

43

from their neighbour expresses her admiration for people so learned, a very special admiration which is determined not to cross the bounds of respect.

When the orator stands up and bows, there is, in the almost exclusively feminine audience, a slight disarray, an awakening, they stretch themselves, as though it were the end of Mass, and the file-past begins. Congratulations, congratulations. . . . Should I say to myself : 'How many women does this lecturer know?' or else 'How many lecturers do these women know?' . . .

A 'lovely listener' cuts through the crowd, goes straight up to the speaker and, from the height of her serene ignorance, her impudence which deserves to be punished, calls out to this man with the youthful silver hair, who is charming, famous and witty 'Compliments, dear master! Yes, yes, very good, very good, take my word for it! A good point, you know, a good point!'

Restaurant Music

The atmosphere of contemporary restaurant entertainment is well caught in this article. Dranem and Mistinguett were two of the most popular and expensive music-hall artistes of the time. Cocteau drew caricatures of them, the former in a checked suit and small matching hat, the latter dancing the *matchiche*.

13 November, 1913

It began with the Hungarian violinist, the hidden violinist, separated at least by a curtain from the place where people eat : first onset, slight irritation, pleasant tingling, a brooding evil. Half-visible behind the greenery, the violinist penetrated one day into the banqueting room – brushing aside the curtain of flowers, wearing a red and gold dolman, coming forward between the tables and taking up his stand, victor with the vehement sound, in our midst, these were so many stages that he passed through with the impudence of a nomad, and we tolerated him. Today all is lost, invaded, devastated for ever in the noble domain of pure gourmandise.

'I have a famous gipsy violinist,' says the Place de l'Opéra. '*I* have a first-prize-winner from the Conservatoire,' replied a corner on the boulevard. 'That's so,' concedes another corner; 'but at my place they sing in Italian.' 'In Italian!' they go one better near the rue de la Paix, 'You're out of date, friend; come and hear my American negroes and see my tango dancers!' 'And us! and us!' assert the bars and grill rooms, 'We have guitarists to accompany the dances, violins to elevate the mind; we have Negresses, people from Montmartre, Argentinians. . . .'

Next they'll have Dranem, Mistinguett; they'll have clowns, boxing matches; they'll have everything – and it won't be enough to make a restaurant into a cheerful place.

A somewhat naïve invalid who had liver trouble and who was told to drink a glass of Vichy water on an empty stomach, said to himself : 'Since one glass of Vichy water gives me relief, ten glasses of Vichy water will cure me ten times as quickly.' He drank them in secret and nearly died. The first restaurant-owner who, at the moment when diners' faces beamed at a short burst of music, concluded : 'By prolonging this burst of harmony I shall prolong indefinitely the ecstasy of these good people' deserves the fate that our hepatic patient narrowly avoided.

At present in every refectory they hand out the ready-made commodity, like endless pasta, music, music, music. Heavy hands, unskilled hands juggle with this power which is as mysterious as electricity, and release destructive forces over us. Between two tangos, between a slow waltz and a ragtime dance there is no longer even the normal interval – one which should be imposed – the moment of silence and moral darkness during which the brain and the stomach can collect themselves again. One should flee – or else seize by the lapels the least illiterate of the ostentatious innkeepers and say to him : 'Understand, understand then that there is no such thing as cheerful music, if it is not interrupted, varied and assisted by considerable silences! Understand that for the most trivial mind gay music which is gay for two, three hours and more is a funereal ordeal! After the first bracing whiplash of bows, after the thousand stinging mandolins, see faces become set, mouths become silent, see anxiety and musical fatalism on people's faces! You are encouraging not appetite but at the very most melancholy drinking, the nocturnal and gloomy habit of drinking champagne on an empty stomach, taken like absinth without food. You're silencing the conversation of friends, and what lovers have not seen floating between them, cradled on the slow and troubled wave of a waltz, the worst phantoms of their memories? . . .'

A Couple

Le Matin, 18 December, 1913

'Monsieur and Madame will be very comfortable here.' The light-hearted boldness of the maître d'hôtel states the fact, but we can't believe a word of it. Where would they be comfortable, the 'lady and the gentleman' who have just sat down at the next table? Under what azure sky, beneath what fortunate palm trees would they both shed their aura of legitimate boredom and conjugal hostility?

Their chic colourless clothes, the elegance of their restrained gestures do not conceal the expression of daily hatred, which has nothing in common with bad temper or with a quarrel between lovers or husband and wife. They aren't 'on bad terms', they're enemies. Each one reveals, with the ease of long-standing habit, a strong aversion which has been put to the test and dictates their gestures, but no longer disturbs them. They are as accustomed to their incompatibility as the cripple to his crutch, the goitrous man to his goitre.

They are long past the stage of impoliteness and even insult – they exchange 'sorries' and 'not at alls' along with the salt and the bread. But the man's gaze, which never meets that of his companion, watches her hands and follows, from the side, the movement of her hat and its aigrette. She, who seems absent-minded, listens ferociously to the man eating; by an imperceptible pause in the movement of her fork she indicates that she has seen the litte drop of wine which has run down on to his tie, and before beginning to eat again she waits until the man has wiped away a trace of egg from his moustache.

He is eating an omelette, she has chosen a sole. He watches the bones that she removes daintily from her mouth and counts them like so many crimes on her part.

Since they have uttered a few words : 'What are you doing today?' 'And you? . . .' we wonder what outings or journeys mean for such people. We wonder about their idle existence, which is secretly occupied, filled and varied by an animosity which they either control or reveal as they wish. . . . Romantic reverie perhaps, facile variations on an imagined theme? . . . No, for in front of our neighbours' plates, as though each of them feared some poison poured out by the other's hand, stand *two half-bottles* of Evian water.

Physical Culture and Women

Le Matin, 18 December, 1913

'What time do you have your physical culture lesson?' – 'Physical culture has made me lose twelve pounds' – 'Don't go to Professor So-and-So : he's given one of our friends a floating kidney!'

Physical culture, physical culture! They rush for it, they use their bull-terrier enthusiasm and their fox-terrier waywardness at it. They all do it, not for very long, 'just long enough to demolish something', according to the melancholy words of a teacher, who admitted to me:

'I would rather deal with children than with women. A child understands, a child obeys. But a woman – or rather women . . . as far as physical culture is concerned – you can divide them into three categories: the one who can't and moans: "Oh, my shoulder, oh my leg! . . ."; the one who says: "Is that all there is to it?" and goes back to the tango; lastly the one who wants to amaze everybody and first of all her teacher. The last, who can also be called the "serious student", is the worst. She works – she over-works. She practises in secret, she overdoes it. I ask her for fifteen *movements* and ten minutes' practice: she exceeds, doubles and multiplies my prescription. She dreams of athletics, record breaking, and in spite of me she reaches exhaustion, while talking all the time about rational health, gymnastics and existence. . . . Rational! I wonder what meaning they can give to that word! . . . I think that for them it means stark naked or something like that. . . .

'After a fortnight, or a month, the doctor is forced to intervene, because of inflammation, a displaced kidney or hernia, and a poor man like me, benefiting still from feminine lack of proportion, loses my title of benefactor of humanity in exchange for that of murderer, charlatan and crook. . . .'

Should One Say It?

Le Matin, 25 December, 1913

'Will you tell your little girl that Father Christmas and the little boy Jesus come down the chimney? Should one say it or not say it?'

I hadn't thought about it! Yes. . . . No. . . .

'Think now, when you were little, when you were at the age when children put their shoes in the fireplace. . . .'

But the child of a village which indifferently allowed its church to crumble away celebrated only the New Year and did not know about the shoes at Christmas time. . . .

'But it's a delicious and touching thing in our children, this calm acceptance of miracle, and the wait for the divine giver of gifts, and the intimate way they begin to live with the boy Jesus, St Nicholas and the Virgin Mary. . . . Come on then, let them, arrange for them a little corner of wonderment in their lives; your daughter will have plenty of time for not believing in anything any more, and you'll have enough time to undeceive her. . . .'

To undeceive her . . . yes, but until that moment, must I deceive her? So she'll believe in Father Christmas – or she'll pretend to believe in him, and her pretence, if I discover it, will humiliate me. If she believes in it, I can already imagine, uneasily, the day when I shall be forced to extinguish by one word the boreal light which haloes the Christ Child in December, efface his divine footsteps in the snow and melt the glittering frost which stiffens Father Christmas's beard. . . .

No, I shan't tell. For it must be a bad moment when one is confronted by a severe small child asking : 'Why did you tell me a lie?'

In the Train

Le Matin, 26 February, 1914

They've just met in the railway compartment, which an unknown traveller and I are covering with newspapers – two good ladies, slightly out of breath; I tidy up the papers I had spread out so that they can fit twenty parcels on to the seat; I can smell vanilla and fresh *pâtisserie* inside the big bags that are bursting open; there are children at home, lots of children – moreover, I can't be unaware of this for very long:

'And how are your four boys?'

'You could say five; are you forgetting my little Maurice?'

'Good Heavens . . . I'm sorry, I don't know what's happening any more. Would you believe it, there are moments when I have my children round me and I say to myself, "They're not all here, but which one is missing?" And this bad winter with all the illnesses that it's brought me, has finally made me lose my head. In any case the little girls have got through their measles, but the two boys take up a lot of room in the house. Charles has neuralgia when he works, and Georges isn't too well.'

'Is it adolescence?'

'No, he's got suicide mania at the moment.'

'Him too? My goodness, how difficult children are these days! It's everywhere, this suicide mania. We haven't got it at home, but the Hespels have a boy like yours, one of eleven, he says that he's fed up with living. He says that there's nothing to be seen in the world except sorrow. . . . I can't tell you how much he says. . . .'

'Ours doesn't look as far as that. But he's got his own ideas firmly fixed in his head. His father orders him: "Go to school, a boy of twelve must study." "Oh, it's like that, is it?" says the boy. "All right, I'm going to kill myself." He keeps on about it. "You don't want to give me wine without water? I'll kill myself. You want me to get up at six o'clock? I'll kill myself." He plays us up, it's terrible. I've got to the stage when I start sweating simply when I see him with a table knife or a skipping rope in his hands. And what can we do?'

'It's very difficult. That's no new fashion! The Hespels are just as worried as you are. As for me, you know, I haven't got the patience of Job. I think in the long run I'd shout back at him: "All right, kill yourself, you wretched boy!" He wouldn't do it, would he, tell me?'

The good mother hen hesitates, and her protuberant blue eyes question in turn the rain-swept plain, me, the bags of meringues and the unknown traveller. . . .

'Yes,' she says in the end. 'And then if, after that, I found my little boy hanging from a skipping rope, or else with the dessert knife. . . . Good heavens, don't talk to me about it any more, I'd like to be back at home already to see if everything's all right. . . .'

The unknown traveller has given up his paper and I my book. We're certainly thinking of the little blackmailer who's waiting for his mother at the next station : 'Oh, so you've brought me meringues instead of *sablé* biscuits? I'll *kill* myself.'

Children who went and drowned themselves because they were reprimanded, who drank poison because they had been deprived of dessert or because they had to go back to school – how long it is, the procession of little ghosts! But I imagine the shades of these wild children as heart-broken and inconsolable, the children in whom the undisciplined excess of life – wounded pride, jealousy, tears ready to damage over-fragile lungs – this feeling expresses itself by the irreversible gesture. . . .

You can be sure however that before this gesture the desperate and vindictive child has thought of everything, he has worked out, with the lively poetry and dramatic taste of his age, the effect of his disappearance. He has arranged his funeral, the flowers and the tears, the paternal sorrow which avenges him – he has seen the empty chair at table, the orphaned toys – he has thought of everything except the things which are too big and too simple for a child – he has imagined everything . . . except being no longer alive.

The Martyrologist

Le Matin, 5 March, 1914

I want to note here some marks of feminine heroism. Heroism which lacks only merit, and which I authorize you to describe also as endurance, sadism, humility – all polite words to avoid using another which occurs to me. Their dry presentation as records will, I hope, present these traits of elegant fanaticism in a more striking form.

Madame A – 30 years old, fine healthy subject. Went from the Pont de la Concorde to the Louvre, *on foot*, wearing a velvet dress over which she had thrown a fur coat, *lined with silk plush.* As soon as the subject began to move, the velvet of the skirt began to rub obstinately against the plush lining the coat. . . . Forty minutes later, arrival of subject at the Pavillon de Rohan. Exhaustion, knees and ankles painful, breathing spasmodic, coat and skirt closely stuck together, rolled into a spiral and riding up to the lumbar region, eyes staring; disturbing nervous phenomena.

Madame B – age : 37. A weak subject but muscular and stronger than one would have imagined to begin with. Tolerated, from 12.30 p.m. until 7.45 p.m., a hat of the blinker-type, completely hiding the right eye and profile. No other accidents beyond a characteristic twisting of the head, evidence of being half-blind (bumping violently into a piece of furniture, encounter with a horse drawing a fiacre, knocking over a tray full of pastries, etc.). Towards 7.35 p.m. the subject showed signs of fatigue, repeated yawns, headaches, dizziness, nausea. The disappearance of the symptoms coincided with the removal of the blinker-type hat.

Mademoiselle C – age : 25. Unruly subject; sportswoman's temperament and also a collector. Declares her taste for walking; collects at her house the most varied examples of fashionable shoes with the help of which she aims to walk. A rapid enquiry

among the subject's domestic staff has allowed us to discover that
her shoes are fitted (especially for walking) with heels $3\frac{1}{2}$ inches
high; the others (for the afternoon and evening) have heels up to
$4\frac{1}{2}$ inches. The subject complained of pain in her feet, knees,
stomach and back. When pressed to show us her feet the subject
put up a desperate resistance pronouncing disconnected words
such as : 'bunions' . . . 'soft corns' . . . 'in-growing toe-nails'. . . .
Temperature up daily; varicose veins.

Madame D – probable age : 50. Blotchy red face. Shortage of
breath. Fatty degeneration of the heart. Obstinate constipation,
cystitis. Incipient mystical delirium, alleges she can stop, for
eighteen hours out of twenty-four, the humiliating functions of
the body, and trusses herself into a sheath of tightly-laced fabric
which imprisons her buttocks, thighs and knees, lacking any opening for hygienic purposes, and she calls it 'the Intangible corset'.

Madame E – age : about 30. Anaemic. Abundant fair hair,
which she wears curled and waved with care. The subject is
inclined to discreet mortifications and voluntarily deprives herself
of contemplating the beauties of this perishable world. Spent the
months of July and August on holiday at the seaside, refusing
obstinately to come out and walk on the beach. Gave as reason
for her imprisonment that 'the salty damp air takes the curl and
wave out of hair'.

Mesdemoiselles F and G – ages : 25 and 28 respectively. Nervous,
agitated; omniscient and pioneering types. Disposition towards
apostolate which appears spontaneously in fanatical axioms.
Example : 'It's never cold when you have a really chic little
tulle chemise that you can show!' Another example : 'I'm never
so warm as when I'm décolletée!' Third example : 'I'd rather
die than wear a woollen underblouse!'
  Mania for exploration, need to sacrifice themselves in front of
crowds. The two subjects recently undertook to go to Moscow,
in winter, taking with them, in order to preserve themselves from
the cold, only fur coats which were 'really Parisian' (ermine
sheath, with a deep revealing slit front and back and bat-wing
sleeves; a big sable coat without collar or sleeves, the latter

replaced by two slits through which you pass your bare arms. There is a similar gap at the hem-line of these two coats and the two subjects do not hesitate to describe it as 'alluring').

As soon as they arrived in Moscow, the two subjects announced their intention of going to the theatre. Their crossing of the hotel foyer was extremely touching, for the two subjects came forward serene and intrepid in the midst of a group of friends and indifferent lookers-on who begged them to go back up to their bedrooms and 'wrap up well'. They were met on the outside stair-case by a temperature of 24°C below zero and their surprise was certainly only equalled in intensity by the pneumonia which followed.

We now arrive at the case of Madame H, which is strictly authentic, like those quoted above.

Madame H – probable age : 35. Dark, authoritarian, omniscient and obstinate type. Following two or three regimes at the same time : one for slimming, the other to avoid enteritis, the third for clearing the complexion. One day replaced her slimming pill by a tango lesson, did the same thing the next day. Developed a strong and assiduous liking for these rhythmic gymnastics, found it entertaining without seeing any harm. Danced the tango after midday, during the evening, even after midnight. Nothing to be observed for two and a half months.

After this lapse of time the subject complained of pain in the lower part of the stomach and back. Her face became hollow, her skin went yellow. The thermometer showed that her temperature went up every day. The tango-dancing continued, so did the pains. The subject concealed her illness until the moment when she had to take to her bed and send for the doctor.

The doctor found serious inflammation and proceeded to interrogate the subject in detail; she finally confessed that for two and a half months, and almost without realizing it, she had danced the tango for seven, eight and sometimes even *eleven* hours a day, always wearing fairly tight shoes with high heels. Peritonitis. Surgical operation, followed by death.

Brutality

Le Matin, 2 July, 1914

I know a little fair-haired dressmaker who works by the day in fashionable houses, she's sweet, so blond and so sweet that people involuntarily call her 'Mademoiselle' and she replies politely 'You can say Mademoiselle, yes, that makes me younger.' Then everyone is surprised, they ask her if she has children, and she says :

'Good heavens! No, I'm still lucky in my bad luck, considering the husband I've had!'

'Did he drink?'

'Oh, it wasn't so much that . . .'

'Did he have T.B.?'

'No, *he* didn't have T.B., his brother did. I'd even have preferred that if I had to choose.'

'Then what was so terrible about him?'

'We hadn't been married six weeks, Madame, when my husband raised his hand against me.'

'And then what happened?'

'Then I said to him : "Take a good look at me, for it's the last time you'll ever see me." '

'And then?'

'And then I left. That was three years ago. He's tried to get me back, several times.'

'Didn't you want to go back?'

'You couldn't expect me to, Madame, a man who has raised his hand against me. . . . I forgive everything, but not that.'

I also have a friend who's going through a divorce, having received from her husband, in a restaurant, a slap which sounded like hand-clapping in a theatre. And then there is the owner-cashier of a grocery shop in my district, who said when speaking of her son-in-law : 'A brutal man who tried to give my daughter a spanking! I can assure you he had a chair broken over his head! Murderer!'

I don't know the 'murderer', nor the man in the restaurant, nor the dressmaker's husband; but all the same I've acquired a good impression of female dignity. Such anger at the touching of an idol, all over a thoughtless blow or rough treatment, there indeed is a sign of the times. These untouchable women will put up with being betrayed or exploited; they will endure, with a slightly tight-lipped expression or a little tear in the corner of their eye, as the partner, husband or lover, prepares and administers the cunning verbal insult, prepared with venom and at length. As I see them rush away, bristling and offended, I think – but it's true that I'm neither the grocer's wife, nor the lady who's divorcing, nor the dressmaker – I think of Molière's Martine, shouting, with her hand on her burning cheek:

'I *like* being beaten.'

A Parisienne Speaks

Le Matin, 28 August, 1914

If I had said to this delightful fair-haired woman, who was leaving her hotel by car: 'Your beauty offends the eye', she would have been just as surprised as hurt; but I would have immediately explained to her:

'Your beauty offends the eye because it glows beneath the uniform of a Red Cross nurse. Don't protest, don't become indignant! I haven't finished. That white smock, enhanced by a striking blood-red cross, that antiseptic sack, be careful, I beg you, what you do with it: pulled tight here, adjusted there, remodelled by the cutting of a good dressmaker, it reveals what it should above all hide: the charming figure of a coquettish woman. And how many hairs stray outside your head-hugging veil! What attractive and almost nocturnal disorder – for I can

see clearly that your veil is not made of muslin, but of silky gauze
– and you look so much, perhaps quite innocently, unlike an
almost sexless servant, but like an elegant woman surprised asleep,
who didn't have the time to powder her face and rub her cheeks
with the pink stick of rouge. . . .

'Your long car, powerful and silent, takes you to the Bois where
you can breathe in the cool of the evening, and no doubt you've
thoroughly earned it, you and the other ladies dressed in white,
whom you'll meet in the allée des Acacias. Your car, which is
promised to the wounded, is already decked out like an ambu-
lance, but at this moment it carries only you and you are offered,
more than offered, in fact, pointed out to the curiosity of the
public by a glorious uniform – glorious and out of place. I beg
you, keep this severe tailored blouse for the well-lit hospital ward
where it goes unnoticed, white against the white wall. Keep it for
the sick room, which it will illuminate. Don't wear it out too soon.
And when you need an hour of fresh air, don't make your healthy
walk into a fancy dress garden-party.'

On and Around the Stage

At the Université Populaire

The first 'Université populaire' or 'People's University' was created in 1898 by Georges Deherme, a French sociologist who helped to propagate the doctrines of positivism. The purpose of these 'universities' was to spread education among 'the people' and to create a closer link between the intellectuals and the working class.

February, 1914

It's the best theatre in Paris, the richest and the most varied. The Comédie-Française, the Odéon, if necessary the Opéra and the Opéra-Comique supply it with stars, the Parlement and the Académie with lecturers. It has performing dogs and jugglers; it is the only place where mimes speak and where you can see as on Sunday evening *chansonniers* making their debut in mimed plays.

And why do you talk about 'homogeneous troupes'? The production of *L'Ecole des Femmes* brought together actors from the Odéon, the Fémina, the Athenée, round a surprising Agnès, a slim suburban girl, who was touching and new and not even made up under her linen hat. At the People's University good-will triggers off miracles which are completed by the public. For the 'best theatre in Paris' is filled with the 'best public'. None is more avid, none more sensitive. If flattery hurts it, it takes refuge beneath clumsy cordiality, it waits and receives the words of the orator or the actor like precious and tangible things; on the benches nearest to the stage some tense faces look as though they want to pluck a fruit.

It is truly the intelligent élite of a population which assembles here, respectful of the texts which are read to it, courteous to the point of restraining their coughing and their applause until the curtain comes down. Nearly everyone who comes to spend an evening here gives up several hours of sleep. The men and women still have on them pieces of thread, scraps of moulded metal, marks made by varnish or acid. Most of the women and girls

61

belong to the aristocratic Parisian race which has small hands and bright eyes. On Sunday evening, among the crowd which crushed into the theatre and rose up along the walls like water that is held back, there was not a single man who had drunk 'one glass too much'. And the People's University must really be a unique place, where the energy of the comrades who are stage hands, the comrades who are extras, the comrades who are producers, is so contagious that this same Sunday, beneath the slightly dusty appearance of a temporary stage manager, courageously carrying a ladder, one could recognize Monsieur Simyan, a former minister, who was treasurer for the Arts.

On Being a Cat

In the Ba-Ta-Clan *Revue*

This article refers to one of the roles which Colette played on the music-hall stage between her first and second marriages. The revue in question, *Ça grise*, was produced at the *Ba-Ta-Clan* by Georges Wague, the well-known mime who was a lifelong friend of Colette's. The magazine *Comœdia* wrote that in the 'Greek mime-drama' *La Chatte amoureuse*, Colette interpreted the cat with 'the versatile, lascivious and disturbing originality of her varied talent'.

Fantasio, 1 March, 1912

I am the Cat in the box – I mean in the plinth of the statue. On the first evening I was very uncomfortable there, bent in three, scraped here and there by the new wood. . . . Now I crouch down, I'm getting used to it; better : I find something enjoyable about my prison ! It gives me a daily treatment of darkness and relative silence, I'm forgotten.

Like the lover in *Boubouroche*, I gradually improve the comfort of my cupboard. I have supplied a piece of carpet, on which I crouch down like a tailor; it is there that I patiently wind my big ball of red wool. . . . I'm thinking very seriously of bringing a little electric lantern. Half-way up the plinth I can see clearly a shelf where I can put the blank exercise-book, the pen, a glass of orangeade, a crystal tube-like vase with a carnation in it. . . . Above, a looking-glass as big as a saucer would reflect my striped cat's face : blue-black moustaches, eyelids crossed through with a vertical line. . . . A few books, happily and easily chosen : *Mes Prisons*, the works of the Reclus Brothers; but *Latude* would make way for M. Honnorat's report on *Low-price Dwellings*. . . .

How he would envy me, if he could see me, 'my likeness, my brother', the agent who is mouldering down there in the 'fish-bowl' at the Montmartre crossroads! With my eye close to the ill-concealed slit in the door that I shall soon break through head first, I am dazzled by a warm vertical beam, gilded with thick dust and smoke; a scarf passes by and changes the colour of the light; a dancing leg, in pearly tights, suddenly appears and disappears. . . . Behind me, beyond the backcloth, I listen to the shouts of the damned and rolls of thunder; they are preparing the triumph of aviation. . . . Above me someone I can't see has just leant against my ceiling of planks, and my cabin sways to the rhythm of breathless dancers. . . . How comfortable it is, in the middle of this turmoil, how comfortable it is to be the obscure Cat in the depths of his box ! . . .

As I turn round, as easily as a chicken curled in its eggshell, I can raise my head to admire, I alone, I the privileged one, the astonishing shortened perspective of the living statue who is posing on the plinth. . . . Without any respect for its beautiful marble immobility, sheathed in silk, at the risk of making him shudder and laugh too soon, I call out to him :

'Statue, you've got some black on you! Statue, your tights are laddering!'

In this way I occupy the too-brief period of my retreat before leaping, like a stray cat in a painted costume, on to the stage. . . . As I emerge from my darkness the footlights blind me : my covered and padded ears can hardly hear. . . . I imitate – feebly, but who *can* imitate it? – the watchful malice, the demanding caress, the electric turbulence of a jealous cat. . . . Alas! it's a very long time now since I ran about on all fours. . . . And, each time I leave the stage, a breathless Cat running on two heavy feet, with my woollen tail flopping against a woman's bottom, I meet, on the threshhold of my dressing-room, the concièrge's Little Cat, the Little Cat, the real Little Cat who's waiting for me there on purpose, thin, dressed in velvet, striped like a snake.

He watches me go upstairs; his cat's face looks down between the supports to the footlights, as diabolical and charming as a flower with tiger markings. He restrains his laughter, but I know he's laughing at me. . . .

Fashion in the Theatre

Le Secret was one of the most successful plays written by Henri Bernstein (1876–1953), best known for his realist dramas. The play was revived at the new Bouffes-Parisiens theatre, 27 October, 1913.

Le Matin, 30 October, 1931

It's a moving scene, between the two women, one of them so evil and the other so affectionate. The latter only knows how to confide and complain; the former avidly receives the confidence, with venomous attention and a marvellous, destructive lightness. I would like to think only of what they are saying and concentrate only on their faces but . . . but there are the dresses.

There is not only a confounded little blood-red topcoat, filled out with frills, but there's also the skirt it allows us to see, white with innocent flowers in crimson velvet, pulled tight at the ankles. There's a black hat which has a rocket at the back, a hat designed for the hemiplegic which hides half a graceful face from the public. . . .

The affectionate woman says to the evil one : 'You're my friend, my counsellor, don't abandon me. . . .'

Shortly afterwards, in the arms of her fiancé, she will shed calm and happy tears. And instead of losing myself in love and drama, I shan't fail, at each step, at each gesture, to curse fashion in the name of good sense and dramatic art, because of the skirt which restricts the knees, the back which looks humped, and the sleeves which hold the elbows down at the belt.

During the following act, when one of the young women turns away and cries, the curtain of white tulle which is draped over her pink gown will simper with the graceful air of some girl in Munich and appear to say : 'Don't let's come to blows ! There are still some good days for dresses that look like sweet-bags.'

Alas ! on this stage and on others, the élan of beautiful women in love recalls a sack-race, and at its best, the way they walk resembles the awkwardness of a small child who has wet its pants. . . .

There's a Shortage of Women

Le Matin, 27 November, 1913

'Oh, there's a shortage of women ! There's a shortage of women !'

The man with the decoration and the military moustache who is complaining loudly like this is no non-commissioned officer dashing by the most rapid of trains towards the gay times of Paris – he's the director of a big theatre in Brussels looking for young leading actresses.

'There's a terrible shortage of women in the theatre ! Intelligent actresses, oh yes ! there are even actresses with talent – talent and conscience, and keenness to work, yes, but that isn't enough !

When you can't have what I call "*the* woman", the one-role woman, one of the three or four "great" ones, I do as everyone else does, I engage the woman with talent. She acts, she's successful and she even creates a precedent. She's fine, but as she is not the "one woman for this role", this is what happens: she pays in physical exhaustion for the effort of her intelligence, the use of her mental qualities which try to supplement her *gift*. I see that at once, I say to myself, "You, my girl, next week you're going to ask me for a little holiday of four or five days, because you've got flu, or else, at the end of your performances, you're going to retire." The *gift*, the thing we call an artistic "temperament", is something so physical, so remote from brain-work, so opposed to it even! A little slip of a girl like Madame S, who isn't capable of being ready for lunch and can't walk half a mile without moaning, can carry four exhausting acts without weakening, for two hundred performances in a row. If you replaced her by an "intelligent actress", who is, at the same time, a fine strong girl . . . the fine strong girl has fallen by the wayside after two weeks! . . .'

The Movies

Le Matin, 19 March, 1914

This echoing hall, consisting of brick, iron and windows, is only a little corner of the cinematographic factory, it's vast, the 'Movies', according to the professional jargon. For the spectator says: 'I'm going to the cinema', while the actor and the mime say, 'I'm making a movie'.

Footsteps echo as in a station; as you walk you have to bump into and circumvent a strange collection of cages for wild animals, baskets with caged hens cackling in them, cardboard rocks and steps in imitation marble. A part of the hall which has been 'set' brings together, beside the blue Adriatic, climbing roses, the pergola of an Italian villa and a terrace with balustrade where a noble couple suddenly sit down : a lord in purple velvet and his companion in a stiff brocade corsage, who murmurs to him in ungentle fashion : 'Talk to me, come on now, talk to me! We look as though we're waiting for the metro!' The mauve beam from the spotlights overwhelms them, they have black lips and the flashing eyes of mulattoes, emphasized with dark blue.

Not far from them another blinding light illuminates a wired enclosure where two lions and a lioness, dazzled and humiliated beneath so much light, move about in front of a Chinese-type hanging from a Louis XVI drawing-room. The lioness becomes excited, jumps up and falls with all her weight on top of a movie-man whom she knocks over. The man is freed and they open the cage for him : 'What for?' he asks, 'she didn't do it maliciously'. And he remains in the cage.

You're not aware of time, here. In this light you don't know if it's dark or light outside. You don't know if these people who cross the hall and climb up the platforms made of wooden planks are leaving or coming to work. There are men, a lot of women and quite a lot of children; – they are people in a hurry, who seem furtive, and go out exhausted with parcels under their arms as though they were leaving a dispensary; blonde chorus girls, made up for the music-hall which is awaiting them; a young person wearing the scratched boots of an animal-tamer; Chinese, babies used as extras, yawning beneath their knitted shawls; two young girl actresses, habituées of the Paris theatres and the movies. These latter have the cold assurance, the lively and cynical look and the reserve which suit their career. They take a rest on a lawn made of cardboard and a spring by the nervous lioness doesn't provoke a single scream. They chat. The younger one, who appears to be eight years old, says to the older one, who is between ten and twelve :

'Yes, my dear, this time, this is it, I've been taken on by the X theatre . . . it was signed this morning. I'm quite pleased, especially by the way it happened. Just think, to go to an audition, just like that, on the spur of the moment, without preparing anything. . . . Naturally I knew a monologue and a fable, but I'd learnt them, I hadn't felt anything about them,

I hadn't gone right into them. Oh! I'd have got through all right, when you have to get through you always do. But I wasn't feeling too happy when I got to the director's office. Oh, well, I really didn't need to worry at all! Nothing, my dear, he didn't ask me for a thing, not a single line; I was engaged for my face, my dear, for my face!'

Dancing School

Le Matin, 28 May, 1914

A famous dancer from abroad, a salamander slightly scorched by too much heat, is at present training young girls in the art of dancing. On a vast stage bordered by dark curtains it's a charming sight, and I've been wondering why the pleasure fades so soon. Pretty, healthy children in white tunics or striped practice costumes, music that has usually been well chosen, isn't that enough then? It's enough, certainly, for a procession of *tableaux vivants*, for two or three pagan entertainments; it's enough for a performance of mime that's light-hearted, childish and fresh; it's not quite enough, I feel, for the composition of a *spectacle de danse*. People are trying to teach us, here and elsewhere, that dancing is grace, unspoilt youth, the veil that drapes itself in the breeze of movement round a semi-naked body, the intoxicated round, the farandole where bare feet trip over rose-petals. . . . This, they tell us, is Dance, with a capital D, eternal dance. Perhaps we'll succeed in believing it if they try very hard. For another type of upbringing, which dates from a long time back, detaches us fairly quickly from pure grace – which, moreover, does not exclude monotony – in favour of a more noticeably acrobatic choreography. How many women spectators, during the evenings given by the foreign artiste and her school, say coldly to themselves :

'Delightful! But after three weeks of lessons I bet that my little daughter and I could take part very respectably in something like that. . . .'

Our senses are no longer delicate enough for us to prefer beauty to great skill. We want the great skill, whether it is the result of a gift or of much patience. We should derive less pleasure from the malicious and pathetic effect produced by Karsavina if her inimitable 'points', her lightness, like that of a drifting leaf, her whirling movement, like a flower calyx detached and spinning round in the air, did not keep her at a great distance from most mortals. The greatest fame earned amongst us by a famous Russian dancer will not be that of having been a subtle mime, nor of carrying within himself this happy understanding of rhythm, of achieving, when he danced, the illusion that he was dancing involuntarily. . . . We are especially enthusiastic over the super-human aspect of choreography which is inaccessible to normal strength : his insect-like leaps, his fountain-like élan, even his strange embraces which are those of an amorous anthropoid.

It is obvious that the pretty little girls at the foreign school are not being forced into the arduous study of superhuman dances. It is clear that they are obeying a somewhat unimaginative lead which is sometimes wrong, for one could occupy those Anglo-Saxon angels in nightdresses rather better than in making them blow unfortunate music by Mendelssohn into mail-coach trumpets.

But the calm moments of this evening underline and enhance an astonishing moment, that when Stravinsky's 'Fireworks' go off both in the orchestra and on the stage. The 'Mistress of Fire' invents here – perhaps unconsciously – without décor, without dancers, the true ballet of the future. We have come a long way now from the first revelations of Loïe Fuller, a long way from the lily-woman, the butterfly-woman or the bird-woman chained to her furnace, fluttering wing and petals. Against the starless night the 'Fireworks' blossom suddenly from the burning wheels, the serpents, suns and silent rockets; the wheels turn incredibly in all directions, serpents blaze and go out, the rockets burst in pink and green gilded bubbles and this restful, fairy-like performance, purified of any human presence, comes only from a few pieces of chiffon soaked in light. . . .

Music and vision, there is nothing like this – except those paintings which have never been copied, which one hesitates to describe, and which, beneath our lowered eyelids, are the petals, garlands and stars embroidered within the black tent of sleep.

Jobs for Women

Le Matin, 2 April, 1914

They're both blonde – are they twelve or thirteen? – they have small, pale, delicate faces which are very skilfully and discreetly powdered, between the long carefully combed curls of hair. A blue ribbon on their right temple, another blue ribbon on the left, at the edge of the black velvet hood which is fastened under their chins. Their two sack-like coats, which are heavy and plain, stop at their knees, the well pulled-up black stockings allow no glimpse of the skin between their close mesh and the Richelieu shoes with their thick soles shine from much polishing.

Are they false minors? No. The stockings would be finer and the skirt more indiscreet. Little girls? But little girls, real ones, don't walk about all alone in pairs between Saint-Augustin and La Trinité, and don't cross the threshold of music-halls with a well-assured step! . . .

These girls, who have just been swallowed up by the dark porch of a stage-door, are dancers, quite simply. But chance has made them, at the age of eighteen, thin and slight with graceful bodies which do not want to fill out, they are little lilacs from the Parisian garden, and like ingenious working women they have allowed their poverty to be exploited. They're taking advantage in honest fashion of a dishonest vogue, that for the 'child number'. You'll see them appearing as boys with bare knees, as a naïve pair of Dutch children, dressed as Cossacks and Ukrainians, in all the dances and costumes which bring out their boyish agility, the dry precision of their fleshless bodies. Both on and off stage they wear the costume appropriate to their odd station, and they go about wearing short skirts, and looking clear-cut and active; but any passer-by who makes a mistake about them is not mistaken twice, for he is informed by a glance, the sour, angular expression of a scrawny cat. . . .

Times are hard and jobs are scarce; not everyone can become a cashier or a stenographer, even if they want to. . . . In resolute and reasonable fashion these two young women have 'set themselves up' as little girls.

Salons and Public Place

In the Chamber of Deputies

In describing how three French statesmen delivered their speeches in the *Chambre des Députés* Colette avoided any mention of their political affiliations. Briand (1862–1932), several times prime minister, was an advanced political thinker who was liked by the moderates. As a speaker he commanded great respect. With Jean Jaurès (1862–1934), the great socialist leader, he founded the newspaper *L'Humanité* in 1904.

Jean-Louis Barthou (1862–1934) occupied many ministerial positions under various governments. He was vice-president in 1926, foreign minister in 1934, the year in which he was assassinated with King Alexander of Yugoslavia at Marseilles.

March 9, 1914

As I lean over this hollow place, I think of the hot springs near Naples. They boil in one place, and barely ferment in another; there are inert zones which the boiling has never reached so far and never will. One crackling corner shudders and jumps like those places in the hot spring where the dry, bubbling sand dances about in irritated grains.

The light, falling from high up, does not improve any face: they are marked with over-shadowy eye-sockets, cheek-bones and bony forehead. They are similar and different between themselves as they will be later under the earth.

The spectacle is moving and instructive, but not ceremonial. 'No, Sir', 'Yes, Sir', it's the tone of the laity. An ex-engine-driver, when making a speech, does not lack imagination nor clumsy violence in his expression, but as soon as laughter assails him, or invective, he clings to the speaker's desk in the shadow of Deschanel, and with his hands behind his back he sulks as though someone had taken his marbles away from him.

The sound of laughter is coarse, insolent, in no way cordial. During the speech you can hear a cow-like yawn, and the vulgar

75

noise of the chamber; this noise is vast and you wait for something that is still worse. . . . My woman neighbour, who is scandalized, murmurs, 'It's really not a suitable place for women'. God knows, however, that they crush into this stifling place and jostle with elbows and hips, almost with fists : they spread out wider, like broody hens, on the benches. Before the session opened the entire semi-circle echoed with a pitiless female voice, a sharp offended cackle, coming from an habituée who was demanding 'her place' in the front row. . . .

Remarkable snobbery, moreover. Most of the people who are here do not need to pretend that they are interested in Parliamentary debates. Even if they are not following passionately their husband, lover, friend or relative, who is cast beneath their eyes in the hollow, they are obeying a sincere, tortuous taste for politics, in which one sees them so rapidly informed, lucid and familiar, ready in advance for all mandates, all responsibilities and all inconsequences.

An Orator : ARISTIDE BRIAND

He only had to stand up and show his great height and his head, which recently seems to be larger, the cheeks heavier and firmer : silence has fallen and the first words in his low, modulated and skilful voice with its musical charm reach to the very back seats.

Slowly he warms up. His back becomes arched, his arms move, his head hardly moves at all. It is fixed to his high shoulders, it moves neither up nor down or to the side. It keeps that inclination which conceals his eyes from the light; you can only guess at the wanness of a look which retains the same direction for a long time and does not flutter here and there over the assembly. At moments the orator leans forward and the curve of his body becomes symbolic; you can imagine, in a romantic fashion, that the shadow of these shoulders and this large back can cover the crowd. . . .

I wonder at the play of his arms, which are sometimes strongly crossed, sometimes they sweep about and scoop up invisible things from the green tablecloth. It's not enough to say that with him gesture maintains the neutral correctness of words; it anticipates, goes beyond and translates, when necessary, anything that they refrain from saying. Gestures denounce the threat that is veiled by the words, gestures are powerful while words only touch upon the subject, it is thanks to this ample and calculated mimicry that the speech seems to be illuminated with hidden warmth and half-seen light, with a strength which keeps itself in reserve and since it keeps the limits secret, gives confidence that is unlimited.

The long arms, which are often as sinuous as grass in running water, rise towards heaven and sometimes bring together two very small, delicate, half-folded hands, which might seem flabby if they did not make a sound as they touch the table, the hard sound of two metal hooks.

ANOTHER ORATOR : LOUIS BARTHOU

He is not tall and shows everyone, as he speaks, his short face with its mocking nose. In spite of his southern origin he has assumed, to extreme, the oily voice and accent of Paris. His words are abundant, ornate and facile; his tireless voice that is placed high up between his throat and his nose, carries a long way, piercing the din without difficulty, assists irony and gives the impression, sometimes the illusion, of a perfect precision.

The orator speaks in voluble fashion, like the one who has preceded him on the rostrum, and possesses the magnetism of which the reader is deprived. His forearm punctuates, with some impatience, and at the level of his chin there can often be seen, as though thrust forward by an aggressive period, capable of more than one thing, a very short, sharp index finger.

THE PROPHET : JAURÈS

This one is a jet of words. Like the water in the stone jet on the fountain in Brussels, words which cost him no effort seem to be torn from him by a convulsion. He seems to speak with his head, his shoulders, his chest, his fists, his back which is that of an old coal-heaver. There emerges from him a terrible sound, which frightens sleep away. His voice rolls along like a jolting carriage and encounters everything on its way : clichés, lies, talk, even the well-devised period, balanced, resonant and solid, which he rushes through in order to dash further on and find something better or worse.

He drinks quickly and speaks. He wipes his forehead and speaks. He defies a heckler who has said nothing. He cries : 'I' and on his lips that is spelt 'I-y' like a bark. He says, unnecessarily : 'Ah!' in order to take the field and launch into a sentence further on. He states, after sixty-five minutes of resounding speech, 'I'm at the end of my tether!' . . . but it is not yet time to register this vague promise. . . . After that he speaks. He looks up and shows a face resembling a thunderstruck Titan, on which one can see that he has a bristly beard and a soft nose. He speaks; what am I saying? His tone rises to the level of the most prophetic lamentations, and buries us in ruins beneath his voice, vast and tumultuous as the sea : 'Hear me, hear me, all of you! I have climbed the mountain so that you shall hear me! I shall speak the truth, even if it has cost me my life. I rend my garments, I strip the hairs from my face, I weep, I shout, I offer my forehead to bullets, and my breast to the knife, so that I may come here and swear, oh men, that . . . the barometer is going down and the spring will be wet!'

Women at the Congrès

The Congrès, in France, is the meeting of the Senate and the Chamber of Deputies, which together form the National Assembly, in order to elect the president of the Republic or to revise the constitution. The Congrès meets at Versailles and the sessions are open to the public. The occasion described by Colette was the election of Raymond Poincaré as President of the Republic. His opponent Jules Pams was a minor figure put forward by the left wing to offer some opposition.

19 January, 1913

Sincerely, I admire them. Their number is impressive; their beauty, which is frequent, pleases; the noise they make inspires consideration. I admire them. . . . But I would very much like to know what they're doing here. How many women, how many women! My neighbour at the Hôtel des Réservoirs named each new arrival just previously; the world of finance, politics, letters, the society world, in short, supplied famous names for this list; the theatre and even the music-hall had delegated their outstanding stars to Versailles. . . .

And as he told me in a hushed voice, and with devotion, 'It's Mme X. . . . Here's Mme Y . . . and here's . . . oh! here's even Mme de Z.' I said to him, 'I can see that all right, but why?'

'What do you mean, why? But I find it very nice of women, this interest, this passion almost for things to do with the Country!'

Things to do with the Country. . . . I know very well that women have always shown curiosity, a meddling and ingenuous taste for intrigue and politics. That is not enough to explain – I was going to say excuse – their presence here, today. There really are a lot of them. A short time ago in the restaurant they found entertainment and delight in an hour's jostling. Across the tables with their white cloths, the hands laden with rings, the rocket-like aigrettes and the newly-gold hair, fell the slanting pink January sunlight, which makes women and caged birds talkative. . . .

At the entrance to the large room there were gracious poses, falsely hesitant and noble apparitions which raised murmurs, and whose feigned modesty begged : 'No, no, no ovation!' There were calculated, showy arrivals, slow arrogant passings-by which entertained the irritable men and caused the dreary luncheon fare to be forgotten for a moment. . . . It was delightful, already somewhat abounding in skirts, somewhat rich in shrill voices.

At the moment the men stagnate, like heavy oil, in the depths of the vast hall of the Congrès. The women, like the light alcohol in a mixture, have risen towards the benches. For those who were not lucky enough to arrive earlier there remain the corridors, and for lack of anything better they manage to reign over them.

Since noon the women spectators of the benches have registered, and with smiles, the impressions of a sardine who is placed live in the tin, or of a chicken travelling by rail, fastened into a wicker basket. About half-past three I insinuate myself on to a bench, beside – I should say 'across' – a lady who is supporting half another lady, while a third, kneeling on the bench, is half astride the second, just as small children sit astride their mother's shoulders. The din here is like the dry breath of a stove, but these women are used to theatres, lectures, society evenings, and remain as lively as crickets, whereas an athlete with sound lungs would wilt like any rose.

Once more I ask myself : 'What are they doing here?' They're talking, it's true. They're watching, with an air of amused courtesy, the dreary procession of men in black who are depositing their voting papers. Then they await, not without languor, the result of the first ballot. Not one of them stands down. Neither hunger, nor thirst, nor any demand of the poor human body, will make them move. They become animated, make forecasts, scribble figures; one skilful one, in the first row, deciphers through her lorgnette the lists of the deputies' votes and reads them aloud. . . .

They're not doing anything and they're not idle. Long training seems to have taught them how to replace action by vivacity and thought by conversation. A name they know is as good as an anecdote to them; they become excited for a moment over a

famous face, as though in front of the curtain which conceals
a show. . . . They say 'Poin-ca-ré' fairly slowly, in three spaced-
out syllables and fire 'Pams' like a bullet. . . .

The end of the vote-counting – the first ballot – sends them
into extreme gaiety, and there again I wonder why. It's not
possible, it's unfortunately not probable that all those befeathered
heads belong to so many ardent patriots, not even exasperated
politicasters, who swear 'Poincaré or death' and 'Pams or exile'
. . . They're women – should I say ordinary women? – whom I'll
see again in boxes at dress rehearsals, at charity fêtes and private
views. But if they seem here to be more aware, more convinced
and more excited than elsewhere, I'm fairly sure it's because
they're more bored. Boredom gives them the illusion of a serious
function which raises them almost to the level of that funereal
man over there on the platform who is ringing a bell. . . .

. . . In the corridors behind the benches there is much chatter.
There are plenty of complaints about so many hours of waiting.
If they cannot get on to the crowded benches, the women, looking important and authoritative, demand chairs, and those who
are walking about occupy the width of the passage, giving themselves the pleasure of impeding the ushers, the frantic comings
and goings of the journalists. . . . Foreign accents dominate in
certain groups, and round about them the greatest names of
France are whispered. . . . Duck-like voices from the American
women, hoarse cooing from the Slavs, all this mingles with the
piercing nasal intonation of the aristocratic suburbs; it's here that
confidential opinions are exchanged at a pitch that would disturb
the deaf, and I notice hardly any more discretion in the gestures
. . . one of them does not omit to draw the gallery's attention to
herself : 'Don't you think it's amusing to meet me? The Comtesse
de X at the Congrès, you could certainly say that was unexpected,
couldn't you?'

No, there's no lack of the unexpected here, about so many,
many women. It's . . . something else, very much to be expected
and difficult to express, a charm they despise and yet a very
feminine charm which could be made up of incompetence,
embarrassment, silence. . . .

Visiting

Le Matin, 5 May, 1911

'Lulu, don't touch that! . . . Don't ferret in the sideboard! . . . *Please*, Lulu, don't lift the divan cover! . . . Good heavens, Lulu, how inquisitive you are!'

I scold Lulu in a low voice, and without success. My comrade defies me in silence, her cat-like face looking over her shoulder, and disarms me by an irresistibly cheeky smile. . . .

'Lulu, it's the last time I go out with you. We are not in our own home here!'

Indeed we are not in our own home. We are in Tunis, visiting Mme Sammama. The chauffeur who leads our party speaks good Italian and acts as improvised guide, cicerone, salesman for everything and also something else. . . . It is he, Beppino, who has taken us into this 'Tunisian home':

'A visit of this sorta is estremely interesting as for artists! The Sammama ladies are very nice people!' asserts Beppino.

But his look and gesture speak volumes about the virtue of Mesdames Sammama, mother and daughter, Jewish women living in Tunis. . . .

Mesdames Sammama live in a French-type house, made of mud, plaster, cardboard and rubble; the absent-minded architect has forgotten the landings, and the apartment of these ladies opens right on to the stairs. If you're very lucky and take great care you can succeed in not falling to the bottom. An old woman enveloped in whitish woollen draperies, with a fichu wound three times round her head, let us in, with no other question apart from a long look from her still velvety eyes, blackened with kohl. . . .

My comrade Lulu can't stand still, utters exclamations, becomes impatient, and the camera round her neck dances up and down.

'Is this a drawing-room? No, it's not a drawing-room : there's a bed. Is it a bedroom? Then why this Henry II sideboard?'

Drawing-room, bedroom, dining-room? One doesn't know. It's an orgy of French furniture, assembled roughly as though by accidental looting. There's a brand new oak buffet, a walnut chest, a wardrobe with a mirror, an upright piano. There's also a bed – and how! – a brass bed for at least three people, strong, expanding, comfortable and swollen beneath a pink satin American eiderdown. Through the half-open door, in the adjoining room, I catch sight of another bed, no less vast, no less cosy, flanked by a further bed resembling the other two. . . .

With a feeling of discouragement I catalogue this 'Tunisian' home. Beige woollen damask curtains hang crooked across the two windows; there are endless calendars with coloured lithographs, zinc pin-trays, *tambourins* painted with Louis XVI landscapes. . . . A thin pinkish carpet covers a quarter of the floor, but by the bed a fairly attractive Turkish carpet has been nailed along the wall. . . . Above the piano, two large photographs smile at each other : a young woman in a tailored suit, a sunshade open above her large beach hat, and a young man with glossy hair. . . .

'We might be in Paris at my concierge's place!' cries Lulu. 'I'll give her a fine surprise, my concierge, when I go back, I'll tell her she's got a "Tunisian" home!'

There's whispering in the adjoining room. . . . The door opens finally for the Sammama ladies, mother and daughter.

Madame Sammama comes forward first, enormous and heavy with the waddling motion of a fat duck. The lower part of her body is draped like a giant flower-pot holder in a *fouta* striped with pink, turquoise green and violet. Between the *fouta* and the little mauve bolero, trimmed with little bows of pale blue ribbon and silver lace, below her short sleeves, you can see the traditional ugly brown singlet mottled with greenish threads.

She comes forward in silence, without smiling, as though she could not see us, and offers us a plump hand which does not clasp ours. . . . Even the audacious Lulu is slightly abashed. But on the heels of Madame Sammama senior there rushes forward Madame – or Mademoiselle Sammama junior, the most charming, the most ornamented, the most talkative of exotic birds!

'Good morning. How do you do? How nice to come and see us! Beppino told my brother about your visit! Don't worry – mother does not speak a word of French. Sit down: coffee will come at once.'

She speaks almost faultless French, in the voice of a little girl; her accent would pass for Slav, or Romanian, with unexpected long and short stresses as in Marseilles. She is charming, neither Jewish nor Tunisian. A short, somewhat retroussé neck, extremely fresh looking rounded cheeks, a wholesome mouth, and brilliant black dancing eyes, the bright eyes of a girl from Bordeaux, a cheerful expression with no veiled Oriental languour. . . . A fringe that is trimmed short brushes against her eyelashes, and a white ribbon ties back a tail of coarse hair, black with a touch of red.

Mademoiselle Sammama has put on in our honour a full pair of trousers – what am I saying? a trouser skirt! – in lilac brocaded satin, a damask from Lyons so good that it 'stands up on its own' as they say in the south. And her bolero is a complicated masterpiece of metal, lace, imitation roses and ribbons.

Conscious of her beauty that is still fresh, Mlle Sammama keeps up a continual flow of words, with frequent laughter, and very Parisian attentiveness. In order to offer us coffee, served in little chipped Limoges cups, she gets up ten times, turns around, shows us her already opulent stern, drags two very small slippers on the tip of her white-stockinged feet, arranges the folds of her wide lilac-coloured trousers and 'acts drawing-room', her hands folded like a real lady.

Lulu is delighted with her and doesn't hesitate to say:
'How nice she is! Like a real doll! Do you want to come and have dinner with us? Or go for a drive in the car? What is that jewel called? And this little jacket? And why are you wearing that sort of knitted waistcoat? And why does your mother have her hair cut short like a boy? Do you mind if I take your photograph?'

After ten minutes they're on intimate terms. Mademoiselle Sammama invites us to a family couscous and we learn that she plays the piano, that she speaks English, that her mother is a little old-fashioned and has never wanted to speak French, that the whole family will sail on the *Carthage* in two weeks, to Paris, 'as every year' !

'But you know,' says Mademoiselle Sammama, laughing, 'I don't dress like this in Paris! I don't want to look like a monkey! Look, there I am in Paris last year.'

She points with vanity to the photograph of the young woman wearing a suit and carrying the sunshade.

'I prefer you in trousers,' declares Lulu, who values local colour. 'What a nice complexion you have in that mauve!'

She doesn't go far enough : Mademoiselle Sammama seems to have been carved from pale amber, without a crack, without any veining; cheeks, neck, arms, in cold velvety flesh, inspire the wish to caress them. However, she simpers and rubs her beautiful cheeks with her hands : 'Oh! you're joking! And I'm so tired! And in any case, I'll never be as beautiful as *Mama.*'

This is obvious enough, and we don't argue. We look at the enormous Madame Sammama as she sits collapsed in a chair. She doesn't move, doesn't try to understand us and doesn't look at you at all. But the back of her neck, her chin and her face have miraculously escaped from the invasion of fat and reveal, without make-up, the remains of a beauty rare in any country of the world. The eyes, which are almost yellow, and strictly horizontal, sleep beneath tapered eyebrows that are barely curved and rise above the eyelids like long thin clouds above the setting sun. Her small, weary mouth has not opened since the start of our visit; only the short leonine nose quivers and indicates disdain, an entirely animal majesty.

She agrees, however, by a sign, to let herself be photographed by Lulu, beside her daughter who puts her hands together like a betrothed village girl, and who has arranged on her full bosom, at the end of a golden chain, her favourite bauble, the treasure of her jewel-case : a little golden mesh purse, empty, a purse which comes from the rue de la Paix. . . .

The Gioconda

The Gioconda, or Mona Lisa, was stolen from the Louvre by the painter Vincenzo Peruggia on 21 August 1911. It was found in Italy and restored to France in 1913.

Le Matin, 1 January, 1914

Barely arrived, *She* receives people, without cordiality, moreover. At the doorway, they read out references with a suspicious eye; it is fair to say that most of the 'intimates' who make their way in are armed, with cameras slung round them and magnesium up to their eyes.

She is there, against a background of green plants. The corner of her mouth and the inside angle of her eyes are both raised, giving her that gentle, suspect, interior smile.

Between two flashes of magnesium the 'intimates' jostle each other in front of her, give her smile for smile, and examine her in detail – for the first time.

'How shiny She is! Have they revarnished her?'

'What has she got on her bosom, there, between the breasts? It looks like a knife wound. . . . Did you know that her lower lip was so full?'

'Yes. But see, my dear, the right hand, which is less in evidence, is so much better executed than the left!' . . . etc.

They take her to pieces, discover her, invent her. They want to love her for something more than her beauty, and adorn her with imaginary weaknesses, she who lacks nothing, and yet has no eyebrows.

A Dinner on 17 March

From December 1913 to mid-March 1914 Gaston Calmette, editor of the daily paper *Le Figaro* attacked the policy and personal reputation of Joseph Caillaux, Minister of Finance in Gaston Doumergue's government, threatening finally to publish some early love-letters he had written before his marriage. When the Minister heard of this threat he said in the presence of Raymond Poincaré that he would kill Calmette. His wife Henriette decided *she* would do so. She bought a revolver, obtained an interview with Calmette in his office and shot him. Her husband, who had resigned from the government, subsequently defended her with such brilliance that she was acquitted. In 1920 Caillaux himself was indicted for 'plotting against the security of the state abroad'.

Colette's possible purpose in writing this article was to give a picture of behaviour more 'feminine' in the orthodox sense than that of Madame Caillaux. The date given here was that of the extraordinary session of the Chamber of Deputies after the assassination.

Le Matin, 26 March 1914

'Half-past eight! . . .'

'You're five minutes fast . . .'

'It doesn't matter. . . . They'll be in a fine state. . . .'

The hostess – wife of one of yesterday's ministers, who will be a minister tomorrow – watches the clock and strains her ears. Only women; the men are in the Chamber, and they are awaiting the end of the sinister session of 17 March.

'There's the bell . . . which one is it?'

'No, it's the telephone.'

They laugh and take bets on the name of the one who'll arrive first, they chatter as though they were thinking of something else and their restless eyes are those of anxious birds. Their preoccupation is so intense that they no longer try to talk; between them there is only a puerile exchange of neo-Oriental kindnesses, compliments about a dress, a hair-style, comparisons between two bags embroidered with pieces of mirror-glass. . . .

'There's the bell this time! . . . It's one of them! . . .' They rush forward and surround the youngest and gayest of the under-secretaries of State. He's wearing a suit, still gay, but weary, his features are drawn and as it were varnished with tiredness and heat.

'Is it over then? Are they coming? Have you seen them?'

For they're thinking about their husbands more than about the affair, the new Affair.

'There's the bell, there's the bell! . . .'

This time it's the master of the house, then two political journalists, a deputy, two deputies, some wearing suits, others a morning-coat or frock-coat. . . . Flushed or sour, they all look as though they have been slightly melted and scorched by a destructive fire. They're hoarse with heat and anger. We hear that they're thirsty, and we feel from their handshakes that during the whole interminable afternoon this warm hand has been handling, with obsessive irritation, a paper-knife, a fountain pen, the links of a watch-chain.

The women who are decked out and fresh, seem to be entertaining exhausted paladins who demand cool water, a basin and ewer, and perfumes. A slender hand slips into the large hand of a man; another touches in secret a forehead below receding hair, in order to examine and cool a fever – gestures of affectionate nurses rather than of lovers. . . .

At table the men swallow the soup like tisane, by large spoonfuls, in order to be rid of it, and then relish a moment of stricken silence. At this hour the most elegant among them is no more than a beast of burden who has just left a cheerless task. The master of the house leans his elbows on the table, unconsciously strips the petals from a rose and says half-aloud:

'How sad, good heavens, how sad! . . .'

The women, however, devoted to their task, know that it is not right to imitate the men's sadness, and that it is the moment for chatter, for the admiring exclamations about the flowers on the centre-piece, about the creamy sauce with the fish; they submerge the gloomy men in a restful, harmless sound made up of youthful voices and moderated laughter, until one of the guests is consoled and as though he were throwing a small log on the fire he utters the fear which sets the whole table ablaze and alters the chatter into snapping. . . .

They're in agreement, all those who are dining here – more or less ! – but they have such an excess of indignation to express that the slightest lapse turns them against each other, intolerant, wounded and malicious; a footman who hurries forward receives in lieu of thanks a very dry 'I'm not talking to you !' just as if he were a member of the Parlement. . . . The voices rise and become hoarse; a woman's virulent loud voice pierces the noise for a moment, then the diners suddenly, and all at once, become conscious of their disorder and of where they are, control themselves, become cordial, laugh at themselves and then begin again immediately afterwards. . . .

But in the end fine food, wines cooled or warmed as necessary, bring an even, slight warmth to ashen cheeks, the gloomy eyes of a betrayed fighter, the pale bloodless ears of a bureaucrat deprived of the sun. Strength returns with laughter, with the desire to please. . . . The guests remember that there are women there who are their wives, attentive to their role and filled with silent devotion, beneath the false court-favourite frivolity – women who are now speaking loudly in their turn, questioning, offering their beauty as a dancer offers her dance. . . . For the relaxation and salutary pleasure of an evening, now they have become simply men again, beneath the tender and as it were rewarded gaze of their good females.

Fashionable Entertainment

Le Matin, 18 June, 1914

To appear on the stage. . . . It seems no more is needed to
intoxicate any number of decent, right-thinking people who
don't live badly, occupied for the remainder of the time with
their affairs, the good name of their next-of-kin, their con-
nections by marriage, of entirely material affairs in fact. One is
assured that the theatrical mania is spreading rapidly and
creating that particular type of monomaniac called the amateur,
he of whom the professional comedian says, shrugging his
shoulders: 'He'd act upside down!'

Watching the well-regulated frolics of an improvised and
wholly aristocratic 'company', hearing around me the detailed
assessment people make of its merits, I seem to discover – beyond
the understandable pleasure of making an appearance, of dressing
up, of prettifying oneself – what it is that brings, then brings
back, then devotedly retains a fashionable artiste on the boards of
a theatre: it is the desire, the need, to be judged by one's peers.

'Ah!' they will tell you at the end of a performance, the febrile
young leading man, the gay freckled *ingénue*, 'ah, to act in a
real theatre, ah, the great public! . . .'

I wouldn't swear to it but I'm inclined to believe that they
are misled by their transient over-excitement. For them the real,
the great public is the 'world'. It is the holy of holies, severe
today, indulgent tomorrow, obstinate rather than austere and
capricious rather than clairvoyant, of their equals, their fellows.
It is their friends, their parents, the uncle they used to hunt with,
the country neighbour, the distant cousin, the pretty sister-in-law,
the fellow clubman, the opulent host, the subscriber to the
Français, the prince and the pretender. . . .

If I am to believe my ears, this 'great' public deserves to be
taken note of, and seems to me much more difficult to beguile
than the other. And what frightful sincerity! None of my neigh-

90

bours bother to consider the cast involved, at this moment, in an antique ballet. Nasal voices override the music, and even friendship itself, on behalf of ultimate truth :

'Is that Mme de X dancing by herself in the middle? Ah, what a mess she's making of it! She's got much too heavy for that kind of exertion.'

'And look at poor Z with his spear! He might at least give the impression of amusing himself! . . . Charming, those little swimming movements of the young people! . . . Oh dear! Tell me, dear friend, why the devil Mlle de B has had the hair removed from under her arms?'

'It's the thing this summer, old chap. Lean forward a bit, I want to say some painful things to your wife . . . yes, to you, dear lady, for having told me that young V was such a pretty boy! . . .'

'What can you expect, I'd no idea that he had knees like a cab-horse! . . . At any rate, I'm sure you like little X, with that tunic that stops above . . . no, below . . . well, her short tunic. She's such a nice child! . . .'

(A short silence, then her interlocutor, at the top of his voice :)

'Yes, not bad, not bad! I got quite worked up about her as recently as the day before yesterday, but now she's showing us so much all at once, I'm not so keen any more. And there's something odd, dear lady, just look at Mme de W, who's so sparkling and talkative at home, she's as much expression on the stage as a wax doll!' (etc.)

For judges like this, some chattering, some tight-lipped, others silently envious, splendid young women dance, concentrating so closely on their steps that some forgetfully retain on their faces the harassed expression of honest employees; splendid young men brandish spears and leap about, a bit stiff at the knees. . . . Against a back-drop the final tableau groups costumes heavy with gold, painted, adorned with pearls and precious stones, fifty figures of men and women self-conscious in their exertions, respectful of a task performed before a public which reflects them like a severe mirror; there are half a hundred singularly varied faces there, whose origins have left their mysterious imprint, here on an aquiline nose, there on a bulging forehead, on a long

English chin, on a suave Saracen oval or a milky brow fringed with red hair – on the rounded cheek and great eyes of a Jewess, dark and magnificent beneath the slow fires of a huge antique diamond.

Streets and Crowds

The Crowd, Election Night

30 April, 1914

Is it, or is it not, the same crowd that waited in the rain, a month ago, for the floats of Mi-Carême? They're alike as two tides, that one and this which shuffles outside *Le Matin* and stays on the boil without actually erupting.

Are those I see here the habitual loiterers who always have an hour, an afternoon, a day to waste at an accident, a procession, a row? . . . No, they are too well informed. They've come here from Montmartre, from Montrouge, they're waiting only for the blue letters and numbers on the frosted screen; connoisseurs, they read the names of remote parliamentary districts and obscure second ballots. . . . The only thing missing from this crowd, with its mauve faces raised to the electric globes, is emotion. It knows what 'it's all about' but, just now, doesn't take it seriously. Worse, it finds it funny. From time to time it applauds a name, for the fun of it; it boos, just for a change. When the interval between two 'final results' is a long one, it cries, in dulcet tones 'hou! hou!' at anything passing by, at the car pulling in with difficulty alongside a swarming pavement; it sings good humouredly: 'Down with the car! Down with! . . .' Finally it attends to its own occupations.

A young man, disturbed by the proximity of an agreeable young woman, shouts all at once, by contagion: 'Down with Millerand!', then corrects himself: 'What on earth am I saying? Up with Millerand! Up with Millerand!'

A splendid outcry, sincere, magnificent, unanimous, greets the defeat of Thalamas. For a moment it assumes the proportions of a popular enthusiasm; a nice little woman pokes her special edition under a stranger's nose and hugs him:

'Thalamas is beaten, Monsieur, Thalamas is beaten!'

'Yes, Madame!' brays the gentleman.

95

He takes the little woman by the arm and they depart in the best of spirits, each brandishing their special edition like a flag.

How gay it all seems, how lighthearted the people who, with laughter and horseplay, disguise and conceal their stubborn vigil! . . . It's political, this ironic crowd, I'd be wrong to think otherwise. Let a tempestuous word or the wind of an affront pass over these thousand mauve faces and they cease to be loiterers, their name is Revolution.

End of a Tour de France

---

28 July, 1912

'Get away from there, you, for Heaven's sake! They're coming, they're coming!' We don't budge. We stay silent and disdainful in the motor-car, drawn up by the side of the road, near the level-crossing at Villennes. An hour's wait has taught us the worth of that warning, hurled at us by passing cyclists. They are red-faced, excited, sweating; they sport little flags on their handle-bars and pedal very rapidly, shouting peremptorily. These are not advance guards, they are small Sunday folk who endeavour to disturb the peace of the market-garden landscape, but without success.

From Poissy to Villennes the dusty roadsides serve as a carpet for placid families, unpretentious cyclists gaitered with string, a few Sunday boozers. Some of them have lunch while awaiting, like us, the return of the Tour de France.

The breeze sways the asparagus seeds, the onion flowers and the ears of corn still standing, bringing with it the abominable stench of fertilizing sewage.

From time to time a youth scorches by on two wheels, coattails flying, and shouts with the eyes popping out of his head, some dramatic, deliberately invented, news :

'Someone's just been killed !'

'There's only three of the Peugeot team left ! All the rest have had it ! . . .'

The road rises like white flour behind them, like the cloud of smoke which conceals an evil spirit conjured up in the theatre. . . .

But here are some other folk, also mounted on two wheels; no longer red, but a strange yellow, they seem to belong to another species. Their faces are obscured, their moustaches matted, by a paste of sweat and dust; their hollow eyes, between caked lashes, make them look like rescued well-diggers.

'Now those are the serious amateurs,' says my companion, 'the racers can't be far off . . .'

While he is still speaking a low cloud gleams white at the bend of the road and rolls down on us. We are blinded, suffocated; we move off gropingly; a pilot car howls at our heels like the siren of a sinking ship; another brushes by with the daring sinuous dash of a giant fish; a frenzied shoal of cyclists with ashen lips, half glimpsed through the dust, clutch at the wings of the cars, skid, collapse. . . .

We follow, enmeshed in the race. I see, passing in front of us, suddenly swallowed up in thick swirls of dust, three slender racers: black and yellow backs carrying red numbers, three creatures who might as well have been faceless, spines arched, heads down to knees, under a white cap. . . . They disappear very quickly, the only ones to be silent in this uproar; their haste to forge ahead, their silence, seem to isolate them from what is happening here. They don't seem to be competing against each other, rather to be fleeing from us, to be the quarry of an escort in which, in the thick dust, there mingle shouts, horn-blowing, acclamations and peals of thunder.

We follow, nourished by fine crisp flint, nostrils scorched. In front of us, in the cloud, there is the vague shadow of a car that is invisible, yet near enough for us to be able to touch its hood; we climb on the seat to see, behind us, another phantom car and others behind that; we divine the waving arms, hear the shouts that anathematize us and demand that we give way. Everywhere around us there is the danger, the suffocating greasy scorched odour, of fires starting up; there is in us, and everywhere around us, the demoniacal lust for speed, the imbecile and invincible desire to be 'the first'.

Meanwhile the silent racers – modest head of this deafening procession – have brought us as far as the railway, where the closed barrier momentarily halts the race. A crowd, brightly dressed in its Sunday best, waits and cheers; there, again, little black and yellow men carrying a red number thread their way through the pedestrians' gate, cross the track and vanish. We stay penned up behind the gates, furious and frustrated. The dust cloud momentarily lowers to let me see a triple file of impatient and powerful cars, the colour of the road, the colour of mud, with masked brick-coloured drivers, which stalk the car in front, all set to pass with a possibly fatal swerve. . . . On my right two men are standing up in their car, outstretched like gargoyles above their driver's head. In the car on the left another man, black with oil and grease, squats on his heels, feet on the cushions, and darts glances over the road from his bulging glasses. They all seem ready to leap, to strike, and the lens of many a photographic apparatus is levelled uneasily like a black gun. . . . It's hot. A stormy sun broods over all this impersonal ferocity. . . .

The whole length of Poissy, a cordial, jovial crowd awaits the racers whom we are now catching up. A fine sturdy old fellow, a little tight, wishes to show his enthusiasm by embracing one of the black and yellow automata, passing at a slowed pace; the faceless automaton suddenly plants a terrible fist in the stout fellow's bloated face and re-enters his cloud like a god avenged. . . .

Avenue de la Reine, on to Boulogne. . . . The crowd, denser than ever, has invaded the middle of the roadway and, in its inconvenient enthusiasm, just makes way for the winner, who nevertheless raises his head, showing his exasperated eyes and open mouth, which may be shouting with rage. . . . They let him through but, as we follow him, the crowd reforms before us just as a field of packed ears of grain reforms after a squall. A second rider brushes against us, equally impeded by the welcoming multitude, and his blond face, also furious, is fixed frenziedly on a point in front of him : the entrance to the velodrome. . . .

It's over. Now there's only the vast track of the Parc Des Princes, filled with a scattered crowd. The shouts, the applause, the music are only a breeze compared with the storm that swept me here, and from which I emerge deafened, head throbbing. But I can still see, down there, a long way off, at the other side of the arena, I can see, rising and falling like the two minuscule untiring cranks which sufficed to stir up this mechanical tempest, the two spindly legs of the winner.

Crowd Impressions

30 May, 1912

The light, a greenish-white, falls from a single central source suspended from the vault of the circus. It beats unpityingly on the ring and the round auditorium; it drives back and devours the shadows so savagely that one submits to it in terms of a catastrophe, rather than as a helpful agent. It takes several minutes for my weak eyes to get accustomed to this devastating glare, and longer still for the halo created by the excessive light, which shimmers – magically violet – around the heads, along the balconies – to die away.

The circus is filled by a marine murmur rising from the dense crowd, which boasts as many heads as an entire town. From the box, perched on high, which I share with a number of film cameramen, I listen carefully to the murmur of quiet crowds, which swells and diminishes but never falls silent; I lean forward as I listen, as if I wished to discover its shifting, elusive origins. Above me, the crowd has invaded the galleries, seems to cling to the walls, and conforms, paradoxically, to the curve of the dome like a swarm of bees huddling under the straw roof of a hive. . . .

The faces which I begin to single out are pasty in the intense green light. Under the blaze of this sad star, the complexion of the men turns a bilious brown or gleams with a terrified pallor. The women, made-up, take on a mauve fuchsia colour; a neck, coated with liquid white, shines like a column of bluish marble. . . . A red dress in a box, another of crude violet, another of emerald, seize and obsess the eyes among the black tail-coats.

Down below, right down at the centre of a pale square bounded by taut ropes, two small naked men suffer the harsh whims of the dismal lighting. One seems quite yellow, darker than his fair hair. The other is a swarthy pink from neck to ankles.

It is amusing, with my feeble eyesight, to see them there so badly, simplified, insubstantial, with their great gloves, like cats rolling a ball of wool. . . . But then I pick out, in the round medallion of the opera-glass, an athletic group so close now that I can make out the texture of the shaved cheeks, the thin streaks which part the sleek hair, and the star of fresh blood which decorates one of the contestants – the far one, the younger – on the forehead, between the eyes, just in the place where La Belle Ferronnière used to fasten a precious stone. This red jewel does not mar the boxer's young still unblemished face, for the match has only just started; the fresh closed mouth, which regulates its breathing, is quite unbruised, as is the careful, short, rather pug-like face of the American champion.

I don't bother to enumerate the blows they exchange. I leave it to an areopagite to assess in points and numbers the formidable choreography which launches them from one rope to another. My place is with this enthusiastic crowd, ill-informed enough to echo with an anguished 'Oh!' each noisy harmless slap of glove against glove, sensitive enough to be moved by a patriotic pro-tectiveness for *its* champion, for the small blond Frenchman, and to gasp when he is short of breath.

I've got a good place, among the film cameramen, whose hands grind away with an unvarying movement, among these empurpled gamblers whose anxiety breaks loose in sudden shouts, incomprehensible exclamations and English oaths, near a silent tense young man who has just unconsciously seized my arm because the blond boxer had fallen to his knees . . . but he gets up, and the hand which was bruising my arm lets go and slips away without the silent young man having cast a glance at me . . .

. . . The strictly measured minutes of pause and combat follow each other. Outbursts of shouts and whistling, directed against the foreign contestant, inform me, without explanation, of a doubtful blow. . . . At one moment the sound of the gong delivers the inert bodies of the two adversaries, in willed collapse, into the hands of their seconds; at the next it resuscitates them, soaked with water and sweat, less white, less young, than they were just now. . . . Is there not, in the widened eye of the blond Frenchman, a tragic and perhaps despairing fixity? No, he still spreads and arches his astonishing back, which seems to protect him completely like a muscular shield. . . . But his impassive, powerful rival is also still on his feet.

I can hardly hear the dull thud of the formidable fists, but they make their mark on the bare flesh and some dumb blow, of which I witnessed only the rapid departure, causes a large bruised flower to blossom on a shoulder or breast, or swells a cheek the colour of an overripe nectarine. . . .

During the intervals the noise of the crowd grows. It is as if – almost silent during the rounds, save for a shout or an acclamation – it harmonizes with the example of the contestants, their brief easing-off, their snatched relaxation; at the sound of the gong it falls silent, restrains its excitement, even the wings of the fans in the women's hands are stilled. . . .

Then is the time to study the changing female faces under the great hats, the pearled turbans! Is it the blond young champion, or money wagered, or the hope of a fatal knock-out that so excites them? The end of the fight approaches and the anxiety of these last few minutes quivers on eyelids emphasized with blue, lips darkened with rouge. . . . To what lover will this woman display that fixed mask, with open mouth and slack jaw, those staring eyes, that face half-dead from concentration? . . . Another woman is all contracted into a bitter grimace; yet another registers the blows with as many morbid twitches. . . . A sudden ageing mortifies them, imposing on them expressions which they will not repeat until next winter finds them round the green tables at Monte Carlo.

True, the excitement of the game, unconscious sadism, sporting fever, there's all that on the male countenances too; but another emotion turns many of the men here into so many immobile contestants, riveted to their seats, anxious – for the French boxer is weakening – stern – for they glorify him as a product of their country – and affectionate – for their noblest vainglory, their most disinterested pride, rest on his victory. He is their champion, the flower of their incarnation, their hope. . . . Will he go down?

. . . The twentieth and last round throws the two adversaries staggering against each other. As if unbalanced, the crowd behind me sways in broken ranks; in front, arms and heads lift irresistibly. . . . A strange rumbling has developed, so deep it seems to spring from the building itself – prelude to a wild clamour; using the opera-glasses with great difficulty, I see, on the blanched ring, the mêlée of two stumbling bodies, the gloved fists of the blond Frenchman striking again and again, no longer with their earlier imperious certainty, but with a blind, tired, almost childish pummelling. . . .

Then nothing more – except shouting. The sovereign triumphal shouts of deliverance, lost at times in the thunder of clapping, then resurgent, dominated by a woman's wild and piercing voice; shouts which fuse momentarily to declaim rhythmically three syllables : Car-pen-tier . . . Car-pen-tier . . . Shouts which spread like a running flame, to which I respond in spite of myself. . . .

The ring is invaded, the boxers are no longer there. Where, then, the Herculean group and the laborious victor of this night? In the ring, borne aloft and carried round on shoulders, there is a great blond child wrapped in a bath-robe; his cheeks and mouth are swollen as if he has been crying a lot; in one hand he holds a small bouquet of roses and waves it at the frenzied crowd with a vague and tremulous gesture, with the smile, so full of weakness, of a convalescent. . . .

The Cemetery of Montmartre

6 November, 1913

This is a place that lacks mystery, but not surprises. The crowd, the flowers, the tired children dragged along – there reigns here a Sunday animation that is hardly contemplative. All these people give the impression of having come here cold-bloodedly, like myself, without 'knowing' anyone. No funereal majesty falls from the pont Caulaincourt, which vibrates with the passage of lorries and buses. It is merely a rather queer kind of garden, a dwarf city with maisonnettes, chapels like cabins and hut-like mausoleums, all in massive stone, iron, marble, cast or hewn in an unruffled bad taste, a childlike vanity which are not disarming but which evoke a shrug of the shoulders or an irritated laugh, and turn this ritual excursion into an indecorous recreation.

What is one reminded of, before this bastion in glazed chocolate, decorated with mouldings, pierced by ox-eyes, if not the entrance to Magic City? And these hoops of yellow stoneware, threaded through the bars of the grilles, against the granite cubes! These ceramic circles are to be found on nearly every tomb here; the living cast them at the dead like circlets of hard gilded bread which the toothless lipless mouths can no longer crunch: 'There! Here's another one! And catch this one! And next year you'll have one more! . . .' One can't give them all real flowers, it would take too many. In this cemetery alone there are so many, so very many dead! They encroach on the paths, they jostle one another, they halt the living, stomachs suddenly gripped between two grilles that almost touch. . . . But the living man or woman cares nothing for this: he frees himself with the same little irritable skip, the same flick of his coat, as he would show in a big store on a crowded day. . . .

Yes, so many dead. . . . Beneath this bridge, at the roadside, next to us, among us; dead so close, so lightly clad with wood, with lead and earth. . . . The wood crumbles, the lead wears into

103

holes, the earth breathes. . . . I don't shudder, but I suspect the thick soil that clings to my shoes, I suspect the smell of the wind; I am revolted by the idea of a licensed charnel-house, allowed in the centre of the town, blatant between a new hotel and a cinema. . . . Why the charnel-house when we have at our service, obedient, joyous, ready to leap forth, to destroy, to purify, to disperse our hideous remains, we have Fire . . .

But then what would become of the 'cult of the dead', as understood by that worthy woman standing in her small enclosure and tapping with an authoritative heel one, two, three, four couched slabs, engraved with names and dates? Simply, she hangs her fur 'animal' round the neck of an urn and scratches off the moss, sweeps, pinches a late rose sucker, mutters to herself and clicks her tongue: 'Tt . . . tt . . . ah! these servants . . .' Then she collects her 'animal' and her gloves, assures the stability of her hat while peering into the bulging medallion within a circlet of pearls, and departs, after a scandalized glance at the ivy, thorns and brambles which, freely and lovingly, are strangling an abandoned green tomb.

The Coffin-Seller of Ghent

Le Matin, 27 November, 1913

We had told the taxi-driver: 'Drive us around for an hour.'

But now night is falling over Ghent and we can see, black against a cold green sky, only the silhouette, deprived of colour, of the old churches, the steeples, the regular zig-zag of the stepped gables; we circumnavigate a pair of pepper-pot turrets, a couple one might think almost oriental with their strange proportions and their inordinate slated hennin. . . .

Tiny, we circle under the giant flank of the château, a geometrical mountain on the peaks of which there still gleam a little new tiling and the white patchwork of recent repair-work;

we skirt a stretch of dark water where a snake of red fire swims slackly. . . . And night closes in. Nothing else, there's nothing else for us but the deserted street, the black façades, and the bright windows – this one, where the cigars and cigarettes are made of chocolates, perhaps, and the granular brown tobacco of fine caster sugar? . . .

Nothing else for us foreigners but shops without customers – shoes, beribboned *charcuterie*, and that other shop there, ablaze behind its well-polished windows, the most beautiful shop, which holds something to satisfy us. For there one finds massive oak, light or dark, modern varnish, rare essences, inlays of copper and silver. . . . Furniture? Yes, if you like. The door is open and brings to us the invigorating odour of new wood, wax polish and fresh shavings; during the half-hour that remains before our train leaves we can choose the most solid, the most elegant, the finest . . . coffin.

There they are, open, illuminated, comfortable. The wide space for the shoulders is very evident, then the box narrows for the long imprisoned legs. . . . Here the adornments of death are prepared and displayed with a Spanish ostentation, man's last stiff bed is exposed quite quite plainly to the street, how the placid beer-seller would laugh at our little romantic shudder! During the day children play outside the shop and I can imagine their likely conversation as they squash their pink noses against the glass: 'I want that one there!' – 'Me for the fine varnished yellow one with handles like a commode, that's the one I'll have when I'm grown-up!'

The Little Shops

Le Matin, 25 December, 1913

Nothing really new in the little shops on the boulevard. The shoe-polish is supreme, the mother-of-pearl stud for a detachable collar is at its post, like the everlasting nougat and the visiting-card while you wait. A *bonbon américain* makes it worth waiting the time it takes to fill, then to empty, in great insubstantial mouthfuls, a cornet of expanded maize rolled in warm honey; – precious innocent bonbon, made without handling! The gold-fish turns – as for two winters now – in its round iridescent bowl, which does not exist, a glass bubble created by the gyration of a scrap of tin-plate. . . .

One buys something for all that, one loiters, but it's very cold. Shoes, the hems of skirts, whiten with dry dust as if it were the middle of summer. Women, little girls, display a supreme hardihood towards the cold, there's hardly an ill-clothed poor devil, this winter, who isn't better covered than an elegant woman : short dress, no shift, muslin stockings and skimpy shoes, three inches of fur at the neck, thus they trot at five degrees below zero without perishing. So much the better.

Near the Opéra, round a hut, there is a small engrossed group where no one shivers or stamps his feet. These are the players of one sou roulette. You can only win sweets or oranges – the prize is unexciting, it's the game that counts, the game in all its beauty. The people who play here don't want to win, they want not to lose. A first sou – another, then another. . . . The two soldiers with hands black with cold, the pale youngster, the man with the grey moustache, the errand-girls arm-in-arm, all those who have stopped here suddenly fall silent, patient, impervious to the frost. They follow the spin of the coloured sectors, the tripping of the pliant whalebone against the nickel-plated barrier. Several have the remote expression, dulled and mild, of sleepers who have kept their eyes open. . . .

During the quarter of an hour we spent there the itinerant croupier regularly took in six sous a minute.

The Wind

Le Matin, 26 March, 1914

It's blowing a gale, with an accompaniment of the lively music of broken window-panes, slamming doors and rattling ironwork; a slate flies and falls flat on the pavement like a slap in the face; a thousand minor catastrophes make a holiday racket; half a window falls from my room to the joyful sound of its shattered panes, while its net curtain, ripped off, flies away like a seagull. . . . One laughs at it, one also laughs to see the indignant cats running, hair on end, the wind at their heels. All this would have no tragic or even serious aspect if one did not hear up aloft, higher than our heads and roofs, an immense booming like the surge of the sea, which swells and subsides like the waves, the free and terrible booming of the wind. Up there a giant breathes; down below wicked goblins are at work, smashing the glass, scattering ashes, tugging at skirts. . . .

A hunched and furtive crowd struggles in the streets; they don't know whether to make a joke of it or flee. It's laughable enough, a hat rolling along, a cape becomes a sail; but there is less cause for amusement by a wrecked cottage on one of the outer boulevards. On the pont Caulaincourt a great cart-horse suddenly comes to a halt, bewildered, brought up short *by the wind*.

'Perhaps he can see it?' says a small girl.

The women are worth looking at. I don't mean those whose occupation or condition obliges them to run before the squall, head lowered, hands on hat or clasped in the woollen shawl. There are others. There are those who, observing the cyclone's ravages, say 'My God!' and mourn the stripped fields, tremble for the sailors, and understand, conjure up the actuality of a tempest. . . . But just now the storm is upon us. Though aware of its sovereign presence, they *do not admit it*, any more than, dressed in a tulle blouse and clad in muslin stockings, they have admitted the January cold. I can see, whirling like autumn leaves, the more flimsy hats, those fur boas which are flung carelessly round the neck without fastener or ribbon, spring capes which flap like flags, even muffs and handbags. The details of this grotesque fashion, which has anticipated neither rain nor wind, nor walking, become odious today, and far from evoking pity the women's distress assumes all the appearance of a punishment. What remains of the windmills of ribbon stuck on the top of those brimless hats? What remains of the ostrich plumes and the bunches of feathers and the tufts and the *plateaux Niniche*?

Huddled against the parapets of the bridges, scudding along the walls, frantic in the middle of a crossroads, they exhibit the graceless immodesty of women who no longer have anything 'underneath' and in whom, despite the expensive stockings and fancy footwear, the sad poverty of black material is turned up to bare flesh on a black, grey or violet leg, without a thread of lace, without a line of hemstitched linen.

In the avenue de la Grande-Armée I overtake a young woman in calling costume, black fox and large hat with osprey feathers. The hat is over one shoulder, the fox drinks at a little lake, the skirt is closely wedded to a muddy cartwheel. And the young woman, dishevelled, fuming, sheds the tears of a maiden fallen into the hands of ruffians, crying: 'It's too much! Oh, it's too much!', quite ready to call a policeman or lodge a complaint at the police-station.

They're Destroying Passy

Le Matin, 4 June, 1914

They're destroying Passy. What remained of a peaceful provincialism, of an unobtrusive bourgeoisie, proud of its streets without shops and its gardens of the rich, what was left of Louis XVI pavilions, or near-centennial Swiss chalets whose flimsy wooden balconies seem to be stayed by hardy wistaria, adventurous virgin vines, is crumbling under picks and pickaxes. The demolition men have an easy job; it is enough to undermine the corner of a balcony, an antiquated verandah, for the whole ramshackle structure to collapse like a soufflé under a spoon.

For us, threatened neighbours, this begins with delightful surprises : behind a stretch of black wall, behind a maisonnette with barred windows, shut up and musty, there appears a deep imprisoned garden, a circle of lime-trees, green relics of a former park, an ornamental lake crowned with midges, the blue slab of a sundial, an old swing with a back to it. . . .

Elsewhere the gaps have exposed a narrow pathway which bisects a curé's garden, and the carts crush the lettuces, the leeks and rose-trees, strip the branches of espalier-trained pear-trees, and loosen, alas, the generous arms of a vine which bears bunches of grapes already set. . . . The navvies chew sprigs of lilac and their heavy horses move off with an iris in their blinkers. It is a gay enough pillage, against a background of walls ripped open to expose to the light the coarse pattern of their irregular cells. Chocolate or purple wallpaper, paintwork of a funereal red, plaster coffering and stucco statuettes, evidences of an epoch when what was ugly became distinguished and when colour was dismissed as an impropriety. . . .

The tragedy begins only when they pull down the arbours. Twenty-four hours, and the quincunx is a builder's yard, the scalped grove trails its tresses in the rubbish, the shrubbery lies helpless under the cries of shelterless birds. Twenty-four hours to ruin the living product of fifty or a hundred years, the tree, the fine old tree which cannot be purchased, the tree which no millionaire can create, or carry away or load, the ancient tree, pride of those sedentary ones who deserved it from watching it grow. . . .

Under the blossoming branches the woodmen are almost invisible. But the entire foliage quivers briefly with each stroke of the axe until the moment when the tree falls. When it has fallen, it still remains so fresh, so stiffly green and so full of sap that one is unaware that it is dead. But the following day, at dawn, there comes to us the odour of the bruised leaves, which wilt and lose their lustre, that odour which is linked with memories of summer holidays, decked and verdant triumphal arches. . . . It is the same odour as rose from the ravaged gardens of Salammbô, trampled by the barbarians, it is the odour which reduced the peasants to tears when their Lord's hunt had passed over the crushed juicy harvest. . . .

Around the Holes

On the 15 and 17 June, 1914, in the place Saint-Augustin, boulevard Haussman and place Saint-Philippe-du-Roule, the ground caved in along the excavations dug for the construction of the underground railway line Porte de Saint-Cloud-Opéra. The number of victims rose to twelve dead and seventeen injured.

Le Matin, 18 June, 1914

Paris, soaked, begins to sink. The fragile crust on which are erected, with such engaging rapidity, sky-scrapers, iron halls, foreign banks with massive façades, railroads, timbering and omnibuses, is breaking up, Oh surprise! to reveal its narrow margins, eroded like those of a lump of sugar soaked in coffee. The Parisian flings out his arms and exclaims: 'It's unbelievable!' A phrase conveying more of surprise than of indignation, and one which takes to task, not so much the unconcerned engineers or the greedy contractors, as Paris, Paris itself, in which the Parisian has placed his trust for so long, Paris which is untrue to itself!

'It's unbelievable!' And, in fact, he does not believe in it. The crowd throngs in dense swarms at all the points of subsidence. It jibs at the 'Move along there, messieudames, move along!' as if it were a patently annoying proposition.

'Why, it's not a crime to look at a hole!' protests one adolescent leaning shiftily on a rope barrier near the Printemps. From where he stands he can easily see the edges of the hole and splinters of wood and the plaster debris which each tremor causes to trickle gently downward, but the idea of danger, of imminent danger, does not spring to his mind any more than to that of the stubbornly curious individuals standing on the waves of the rue Tronchet and the undulations of the boulevard Haussmann. The spectacle of what remains is more disquieting than the appearance of what the catastrophe has destroyed – the catastrophe is just another hole! – this suddenly rippled earth, these rails broken like straws, these long human exertions jeopardized or obliterated in an hour, it's enough to evoke disquiet, distress, defiance from an entire population, but *another* population. This one, preserved by its very frivolity, forgets and ignores the existence of the hideous underside of its familiar paths, the hidden cataracts, the trembling vaults, the fractured sewer. . . . At most, someone next to me holds his nose when the breeze wafts to us the deathly smell which mounts from the crevasse : the complex greasy sewer taint, the chill odour of a drowned rat, of gas, of damp cellar and clayey tomb. . . .

It is possibly because of this odour that a man near me has suddenly begun, with staring eyes, to gaze at a spot in the pavement at his feet. Then he takes three precipitate steps and bounds as if some animal were passing between his legs or as if he felt the ground tremble. Then he makes another light sleepwalking bound and flees, running on the very tips of his toes.

Solemnities and Celebrations

The Review

Le Matin, 24 April, 1914

I had never seen this before. I cannot compare this spectacle with any recollection, any image already encountered and recorded. An ants' nest? . . . No; nor waves without number. . . . I have seen nothing so disquieting, nothing so totally invasive of the mind, as the appearance on the plain below, very far off, of the first regiments marching towards us. There is nothing which can inspire such a healthy, and therefore admissible, fear as the progress of these sentient parallelograms, at their insensible yet assured pace, sombre, smooth as grass at a distance, growing bigger, scored by a red streak – the infantry – striped with a frieze of polished silver – the cuirassiers. . . . My sight is weak, I've no binoculars, so for me the spectacle is even finer. I can't see the men, nor the minute details, nor the horses in an inflexible line – I see the *Army*. . . . Those atoms dotted along its flank, are they its leaders, identified by my neighbours? What matter? What appeals to the most disinterested, the noblest elements, is the mysterious beauty of human movement in prodigious masses; it is the attraction of number, of a rigid geometry which suddenly dissolves, of an obedient multitude which inscribes legibly, on the flat plain, the arabesques of defence or attack, the idea of some quite minor commander, hidden somewhere.

It's all the same to me that 'Saint Cyr' marches swinging a left hand which 'Polytechnique' holds stiff and still; and I distinguish the dancing step of the Zouaves only because it creates two wings of white dust at the feet of the 4th regiment. . . . The ranks of the line I could wish inexhaustible, that I might the longer enjoy the impeccable choreography imparted to the long columns of men by the fine light step of the French infantryman.

Sombre blue, gay red, black stuck with silver, I have here, before my eyes, a sizeable portion of our army. . . . With my emotion there rises a barbarian, a possessive desire towards this mobile abundance; one would, at least, like to dispose of the master-word, the unheard command which, before our eyes, controls this army, tests its infinite flexibility, its thoroughbred pace, groups and disperses it, arranges its fragments in a precise mosaic, causes a rectangle to blossom into a fan, and magically projects, in the form of a bold thin line, the substance of two massive squads of cavalry. . . .

The rising wind blows the dust, masking battalions here, revealing breastplates there, elsewhere the drooping stalks of a harvest of bayonets; the grand thunder, the brief pink flash of the guns, the crackle of the machine-guns, the breathless outbursts from the bands, the piercing trumpets, all this stirs in the spirit perhaps the most ancient of human joys, the joy of service and combat. . . . The spectators in the stands will not forget, any more than I, the heroic air, restrained yet audible, which accompanies the brass, murmured by a thousand half-closed mouths:

Mourir pour la patrie. . . .

The next moment an overwhelming cloud rolls before us – smoke, dust, the steam of streaming flanks – bearing the last charge, the Charge, divinely cloudlike, human in the guessed gleam of a breastplate, the dash of an arm and a sword piercing the murk, the recurved collar and flying hooves of a horse wild with ardour. . . .

They're here, They're here!

24 April, 1914

Paris, enchanted, is awaiting a king. Nothing is lacking from its republican joy; it will have a queen to acclaim, as well as a monarch. It has flags, soldiers, military bands; it has sunshine, dust, and the opportunity to play truant for a long afternoon in midweek.

Better still, it is almost the 14 July, and a wealth of natural flowers on buildings and in the baskets on the lamp-standards replaces the painted streamers and sad cardboard escutcheons. It is a new joy, undimmed and undiminished by any anniversary; it is a sudden outburst of warm-hearted confidence that brings into the streets, for a triumphal hour, a populace rather surprised by its own excitement, astonished at being so numerous and so enthusiastic. The rue de la Paix vibrates with flags and foliage, the red of the banners imparts a sanguine reflection to the walls, electric arches shine in broad daylight, floral rigging seems to sway the entire avenue de l'Opéra like a decked-out junk, and a storm-cloud advances above the city like a canopy of dark blue rimmed with fire.

At the corner of a pavement I find myself imprisoned like an ear of corn in a cornfield. In front of me three rows of heads and shoulders, then the blue backs of the police. Behind me a double ladder, at so much a rung, which bends under a very elegant feminine burden – taffeta, pearled slippers, ospreys, ribbons, cherries. . . . Has one seen ladders so preciously laden since the visit of the Russian sovereigns? . . . A plumber's tool-bag presses hard against my right side; on the left, a well got up young man endeavours to engage in conversation with a viperine errand-girl, acid and indomitable. . . .

'Excuse me, Mademoiselle, is King George due to arrive at 4.30 p.m.?'

'I don't know anything about that!' replies the errand-girl, 'He's due to take me out for a drink at 6 p.m.'

117

All my neighbours display patience, not much excitement, good manners, and comparative verbal respect; but they stay here and won't budge until it's all over. The ladies of the ladder seem to be as preoccupied with the English sovereigns as they might be with a sensible skirt, and only reveal by the little intimate stories they tell each other at the tops of their voices that they probably belong to high society.

'The Breteuils' dinner-party will be rather a frost!' one of them shouts.

'Why is that?' yelps her neighbour below.

'Because Princess M and the Duchess of L have both been invited, they're both going, and they can't stand one another!'

I hear, without seeing, the first part of the escort and the first landau, their passage greeted peaceably in our corner of the crowd and remarked on briefly by the errand-girl:

'It's nothing, it's Hennion. . . . It's nothing, just a general. . . .'

'My dear,' ululates one of the ladies of the ladder, 'what shabby landaus!'

'Those chaps in cocked hats and feathers,' remarks the errand-girl, 'they don't seem to realize that ostrich feather fringes aren't being worn this year!'

But suddenly she turns pale and, tight-lipped, dances up and down, then shouts wildly:

'Here they come! Here they come!'

'Here they come!' repeat the ladies of the ladder, the previously taciturn plumber, the fatuous well got up young man, craning towards arrivals whom I can't yet see. . . .

'Long live the King! . . . Long live the Queen! . . . Long live England! . . .'

The yelping ladies, the pallid and ecstatic errand-girl, who has two tears at the end of her lashes, the plumber who cheers without abandoning his fag-end, my neighbours so insignificant and indifferent till now, all give tongue, raise their hands, wave handkerchiefs, each darting his little personal flame to quicken the fire of popular enthusiasm, brief, designedly ironic, familiar or respectful, everywhere sincere, and self-critical out of sheer self-respect as soon as the procession has turned the corner of the avenue :

'Not bad, that, not bad!' opines the errand-girl, still husky with emotion. 'There's just one thing they could do without : Queen Mary's blue hat.'

NIGHT : THE ILLUMINATIONS

A crowd is a fine thing. This one, enlivened by bright hats and female faces, flows with a tide so slow that its current is barely appreciable, under the coloured lights of the rue Royale. On the place de la Concorde two hundred or more motor-cars are stuck in an invisible glue. No impatience, we settle down for a space of time, side by side, as if on an English river. Families coalesce, the young people exchange cigarettes, children perch on the turned-back roofs of the landaulets . . . Behind us there is a great open expanse of April sky, dark, starry, cut by the fountain of milky light that falls from the Eiffel tower.

The illuminations. . . . Well no, it's not that. The houses of the rue Royale, behind their twin electric stream, fall into massive shadow that conceals their flapping flags. The boulevard, dim here, lit up there, has only touches of light. The avenue de l'Opéra has not switched on its festoons and is as dark as the day after a holiday. The rue de la Paix is an easy winner, and there we learn what was and what wasn't the right thing to do. A little more of the 'entente cordiale' among the tradespeople, a little collaboration in decoration, a little submission to a guiding spirit, which was lacking, and Paris would have glowed with a concerted blaze, evenly distributed, blue and yellow like the three windows of this clever businesswoman, for instance, or the blush of dawn, all showers and rivers of light in sparkling emeralds. . . .

New Year Party

28 December, 1911

It must be quite four o'clock, half-past four. . . . I don't know for certain, I say as much from the state of the flowers, and the women, at the tables. . . . The flowers are half-dead, scentless, limp and tepid to the touch. The women, very much alive, won't lose their looks until daybreak : a good foundation cream guarantees almost all of them, the night through, the luminous somewhat febrile pink of certain hydrangeas. Some of them have been drinking and grow pale; others, who have been embraced too often, display a spot rubbed red by a nose tip in the middle of their powdered face. . . .

The noise is unendurable. I defend myself against it mechanically, clenching my teeth and closing my eyes. A happy New Year cannot dispense with rattles, tambourines, trumpets, whistles and sirens. . . . Yes, I think it really must be half-past four, the men's shirt-fronts are so crumpled. . . . Everyone's stopped eating; they're still drinking a little because they're shouting. But you wouldn't find, among the two hundred women having supper in this long room blazing with light, a single one who is really drunk. At a closer look I might possibly discover a quiet male boozer, quite tight, who's no trouble to anyone. . . .

The air is blue with smoke and dust, the dryness is suffocating : many women cough unconsciously. . . . Down there, at the end of the hall, a swirl of ospreys, of swaying birds of paradise, of spangles, indicates a little scuffle, whose shouts and laughter do not penetrate the general hubbub. . . . I suffer the clamour, the rattles and the music with an almost pleasurable feeling of fatigue and powerlessness, as when one is on the seashore on a very windy day. . . . A trumpet blast in the ear or the tickling of a bundle of streamers evoke in me a defensive grimace, unless I stir myself and shout, from contagion, with the others. . . .

It must be late. . . . The men remain calm enough, doubtless

120

because the women are losing patience. I can see some prancing where they are, standing between the closely-packed tables. Some, seated, and swaying their heads and shoulders like animals on the leash. The majority stifle a little in their tight dresses and, to cool themselves, imitate with their elbows an awkward beating of wings. . . .

Right next to me a blonde devilish young woman untiringly improvises dances with her arms, trunk and rump. Despite her split tunic, which reveals in the hollow of her back a little skin and fine linen, she is not immodest for she smiles with an absorbed air and seems to obey an inward music. She has just sat down at last, all moist with sweat, and her shot silk dress smells like a soaked silken umbrella. Her friends applaud her; she buries her fresh face and begins to laugh, just as she danced, for herself, for herself alone, in a knowing and mysterious manner that sets her apart from us. . . .

It's stifling. It rains hats of crinkled paper, tangerine peel and streamers. The noise increases. No conversation, even shouted, is possible; the monotonous racket lacks precision, stars and gaiety : what's needed here is a New Year's master of ceremonies, duly appointed. The very excess of lights above, below, in festoons, outlining doors and windows, is more stupefying than enlivening. . . .

Look, there's someone who's happy, that blowsy, middle-aged woman there. . . . She has given up being pretty, she has sent her stylish corsets to the devil, and her turban à la Madame de Staël suits her like a ring in the nose. . . . And doesn't she give her face a good wipe with her napkin ! . . .

To leave a place for the dancers in the centre of the room we are crowded back against the windows, and the women diners, who are now standing, offer themselves familiarly to the men in the manner of savages, tendering their neck, a bare shoulder; they have a barbaric manner of taking stock of strangers, of planting themselves against the wall to await homage, or outrage. . . .

Also standing, caught between the table and the window, I empty in little sips some lukewarm left-over champagne. From time to time I press against my flushed cheek a handful of flowers which were trailing on the table-cloth among the cigar-ash and which smell of tobacco. . . . Someone is letting himself go in the small central arena: I can see bouncing about, above the plumes and the paper hats, a young dancer's head with sleek hair and pink scrubbed cheeks. . . .

I feel that I shall never have the strength to get away from here. I feel that nothing will serve to moisten my parched throat. I stifle. . . . Gropingly, behind the curtain, my hand finds and turns the window fastener: a vertical gust of fresh moist air advances like a blade, bringing the odour of the night, of box, of damp pines: a garden is sleeping there under the rain. By plastering my forehead against the black window-pane I can make out glistening laurels, the spindles of silvered pines, and, further away, the obscure swaying of a bare grove.

How familiar this nocturnal image suddenly is to me! Is it the wine and the fatigue that create for me, in this barely visible garden, the sloping terrace and the rickety flight of stairs? Thus it was, forehead at the window-pane, that I once used to seek, during Christmas Eve, a garden asleep under its bluish snow, or under the rain, or all white with frost beneath the stars. . . .

I do not stir for fear of dispelling, at my back, the provincial mirage which rises from my past: a faded salon where the white marble clock shows midnight between two holly wreaths. On the big table the gilt-edged books, the game of backgammon and the box of dominoes have simply been pushed a little to one side to make room for the rum-soaked cake and the pale old Frontignan. . . .

There is also China tea, which I'm allowed tonight and which keeps me awake with rapidly beating heart till daybreak. There is also the cat of three colours, busy, miaowing with greed, whom my mother's pretty voice calls with a long musical cry:

'Minne!'

On the floor there are one, two, three dogs running around, which get a little crushed, like carpets. Everywhere there is the warm disorder of a happy house, delivered over to children and fond animals. . . .

If I turn round, shall I see once more – time for a glimpse, time for a flicker of my damp eyelashes – shall I see all that once more? . . . A hand touches my shoulder but I don't want to turn round. . . . And I don't care when someone shouts, laughing, in my ear :

'You'll catch your death from opening that window, what are you thinking of ? Come, we're leaving !'

I don't care a bit because, as it happens, I can hear as in former days that young maternal voice :

'Beauty ! . . . my shining sun ! . . . My golden jewel ! It's late, run off to bed. . . .'

The Clogs

I never had, when I was a child, a Christmas shoe. I feel a little upset about this now but at that time I thought nothing of it. I am the child of a very 'unorthodox' part of the world, where the unbelieving tomboys and urchins might have said to the little Jesus in person, descended white and luminous by the chimney :

'Just wait, your mother'll give you a good larruping to teach you to go out all bare in your shirt !'

On Christmas Eve I would take off my snow-soaked clogs and carry them, as on other evenings, to the warm range in the kitchen, where they would dry till morning. Now that I'm getting old, I experience a tardy unseasonable regret – a romantic flower, a sentimental and outmoded bouquet – regret for a faith I never had. . . .

No, I had nothing to do with Christmas shoes. I put on my clogs with their pointed toes over my woollen stockings without looking to see, on the morning of that miraculous night, whether they bore the golden trace, the diamond hoar-frost, of a divine touch. . . . They had, that morning, their usual black waxed snout and supple strap. . . . As usual, they clattered under my brisk authoritative step, trotting along in the snow, and slid on the gleaming slides alongside the school wall. . . . They heralded me from afar when I returned home at noon, clattering and capering over the uneven paving-stones, the 'cats' heads' which made the lanes of my little town so dangerous. . . . I used to return quite blue with cold, breathless from fighting and rolling

in the fresh snow, my hood awry, hands red beneath the knitted
mittens . . .

'Colette, your clogs!'

My mother's voice would call me to order when I crossed the
threshold of the dining-room. Docile, I'd enter in my silent
stockings, and until the time when the appeal of the snow, the
desire for play, enticed me afresh, my clogs awaited me in the
corridor, coupled, pointed, with the patient air of two black rats
lying in wait, muzzle by muzzle . . .

How many times they waited for me, cunning accomplices,
until it was time for the forbidden recreation! . . .

At five o'clock, in December, under an almost black sky, the
snow is blue. At the window, hidden behind the muslin curtain,
I would look out at the street. I knew that in an out-of-the-way
little square there twined a silent frenetic chain of abandoned
hoydens who escaped every evening for the intense pleasure of
rolling in the snow, grappling with it, burying themselves in it,
to return home around six o'clock, soaked and miserable, risking a
cuff or a spanking . . .

A nocturnal imp tugged at my sleeve and I soon followed,
clogs in hand. . . . Outside, my eyes once attuned to the dark
would make out other infantile shadows carrying their clogs in
their hands, insubstantial, demoniac, like the young cats of the
witches' sabbat, grey with the icy blast from the east and the
flying snow. . . .

Winter twilights, red lamp in the night, the bitter wind that
gets up at the end of the day – the garden divined in the dark
air, shrunken, smothered in snow, overwhelmed pine-trees which
from time to time let the burden slide in avalanches from their
arms, fan-strokes of bewildered sparrows and their nervous games,
their settling in a powder of fine crystal, iridescent like a fountain's spume. . . . O, all those winter memories, all those childhood Christmases, may this Christmas daydream restore you to
me! May my memories return one by one, falling softly and
silently as petals, to fill this narrow slipper fallen from my bare
foot, before a wild fire in which there revives and is consumed
the image of a fresh healthy child in an apron of black material,
weatherbeaten with cold, reddened by the sun, her impatient feet
in blackened ash clogs, who never knew the clogs of Christmas! . . .

New Year's Day

Le Matin, 1 January, 1914

'It's a parcel, ma'am!'

The friend with whom I am having tea puts down her cup, claps her hands, jumps to her feet:

'What luck! Another parcel!'

She cuts the string, uses a paper-knife like a cold chisel to rip the slender package open, unties the ribbons, teases out the shavings of the backing, and eventually uncovers an iridescent vase.

'There,' she says frigidly, 'it's a vase.'

'A very pretty vase!'

'Very pretty. Maria, put this on the table . . . no, in my room . . . oh well, anywhere you like!'

She sits down again, takes up her cup, and we chat. But she scarcely seems to hear me for she is keeping one ear open for the sound of the bell.

Between Christmas and New Year she waits, the whole time, for the *other* parcel – the one that hasn't come yet, for which she jumps up each time, which is the most splendid each time, the most done up, the most got up with string, casket and triple cardboard. . . .

It seems to me that female joy, around the first of January, resembles not so much that of the spoiled child as the anxious hope of the prospector. At sight of the wrapped jewel, the sweetmeats or the mysterious trinket they are atremble; but chiefly on account of the obstacle. What 'surprise' could astonish them? What gift surpass their expectations? A haughty and miserable young Parisian girl one day saw clasped round her charming neck, under the skinned rabbit that passed as fox, a row of fine pearls, and knew how to answer the jealous friends who whispered: 'She can't get over it!'

'You're right . . . at not having had it before!'

125

A reply like this is evidence less of cupidity than of a bohemian familiarity with riches, with all the powers of this world, and I can well imagine the same little pauper throwing her necklace into the Seine, if only to flabbergast the giver. Tomorrow, when the last blue-caped deliveryman has received his last tip, my friend will begin to *choose* among her presents – it will be a very secret selection where actual snobbery will play no part. And it may be that she will properly choose, scorning a precious cup of jade, this simple glass bubble where a rainbow goes round like an iridescent fish. . . . If I ask her, she won't tell me why, perhaps she won't want to, perhaps she won't know. She will laugh in a rather babyish fashion, vaguely excusing herself : 'Oh, *I* don't know. . . . I rather like that. . . . It reminds me of old times, when I was little. . . .'

I shan't insist; I shall laugh in no less stupid a fashion, while thinking of the perennial strength of certain traditions, of a certain childhood recollection. I shall recall an age when keen sensation lacks words, takes fright at its own acuity, conceals itself. I shan't forget how I grieved my parents by demanding for my New Year gift, when I was eight, a little old volume entitled *Les Douze Césars*, a flask of quicksilver and a travelling rug rolled up in a strap. Could I make simple grown-ups understand that *Les Douze Césars* was not a boring book but a censer whose worm-eaten pages smelled of old paper, a touch of apple, a touch of the thuja of the glazed wardrobe? The shifting of mercury, chill and vivid in the hollow of the hand like a small snake, that was for touch – and for sight when I squashed it with the tip of my thumb into a thousand grey sparks. . . . And the travelling rug, if they'd given it to me, would never have left its strap because it was just in its double leather belt that it signified, for a child who knew only her own village, journeys, adventures, perils, and all those countries on the other side of the world. . . .

To be sure, I would not want my friend to learn that yesterday I yielded to the temptation – in honour of 'old times' and because it was New Year's Eve – to buy a pound of pistachio fondants of poor quality and half a dozen marbles, enormous globes, whose common stuff imprisons a kind of green and pink caramel, with which I dare not play. . . .

14 July

Le Matin, 16 July, 1914

A sparrowhawk, all golden in the sun, planes, leaning outspread against the wind. He is the only moving creature in the land-scape, a little faster than a star, a little slower than a cloud. The day advances and the time has arrived when the sea will sur-render to the sky all the opulent blues it had retained, to become, under the lowering sun, bright silver, then pink. . . . That object, flapping in the wind on the promontory of a rock, is it yet another flag? No, only sea-wrack, I breathe again. . . . It's just that I've seen so many banners today, so many crumpled white dresses spotted with sweat, so many *guinguettes* with faded foliage, so many drunken blouses and reeling aprons. . . . Every village is an open-air bar, hostile to the tourist and the horn that heralds him. Next to the bar, a rifle-range; next to the range, a carousel of pigs or rabbits. A mile further on it begins all over again, amidst the sharp sour odour of cider spilt on the sand, the smoke of fire-crackers and the greasy smell of rancid butter, cattle-shed and fresh linen that emanates from an exclusively rural crowd. . . .

It seems that today every pleasure – for there is hardly a bush that does not shelter a couple – is permitted, save that of being alone. The smallest bay bears the traces of picnics in besmirched paper and eggshells; a dry sandy meadow beside the sea blooms suddenly with frivolous Cancale head-dresses, and from the depth of this bay to the very summit of its rocks I've feared the beating of a tricolour wing, the nasal twang of mechanical organs . . .

But no. This time we are out of reach. The falling tide, at each reflux, sucks at a beach devoid of imprints, slowly empties the retreats of crab and blue lobster. The golden sparrowhawk is not yet on the wane, and its marine twin shows me, distinct, tempting and inaccessible, its brushed-up feathers, its polished beak, and its fine fiery eye which does not contemplate the earth.

One-sided Dialogues

7 December, 1911

'Godmother?'

. . .

'What are you writing, godmother? A story for the news-papers? Is it a sad story?'

. . .?

'Because you look so unhappy!'

. . .

'Ah! Is it because you're late? It's like an essay, you've got to hand in your work on the day they tell you? What would they say if you gave in your book with nothing in it?'

. . .?

'But the gentlemen who decide at the newspapers!'

. . .

'They wouldn't pay you? . . . Now that's really annoying. It's just the same with me; but Mama only gives me two sous for a composition. She says that I'm mercenary. Anyway, you must get on with it. Show me your page. Is that all you've done? But you'll never get finished!'

. . .!

'What, you haven't got a subject? Don't they give you a theme, like we get at school for French essays? You do have, that's lucky!'

. . .

'What *I* would like is for Mademoiselle to let us write down everything that came into our heads. Oh Lord, if only I were a writer!'

. . .?

'What would I write? I'd write a hundred thousand million things, and children's stories.'

. . .

'I know there are plenty of them already; but some are

131

enough to make you sick of being a child. What sort of books are they going to give me for New Year's presents? You know, they take us too much for imbeciles! When I see in a catalogue: "For young people" I say to myself: "There! There they go again! More grown-ups who've taken the devil of a lot of trouble to bring themselves down to our level, as they put it!" I don't know why they have to adopt a special tone, these grown-ups, to bring themselves down to our level. Do we children get involved in writing books for grown-ups?'

. . .

'It would only be fair, wouldn't it? I'm all for being fair. For instance, I like an instructive book to be an instructive book, and I like a book meant for amusement to be amusing. I don't like a mixture. Every year now, in the children's books, there's an automobile arriving, and always in the story there's been a gentleman to slip in softly his opinion on the progress of mechanics. . . . Nowadays you can be sure of seeing a stunning aviator descend from the sky, but he talks about the conquest of the air . . . and the . . . the glorious dead who blazed the trail. Do you see, all the time there are things in children's books that really get me down, things that smell of a grown-up giving a lesson. It's no use papa repeating: 'A child must understand everything it reads . . . *I* find that grotexque . . .'

. . .

'Grotesque? You're sure? Grotexque is much nicer.'

. . .?

'I find that grotexque because grown-ups never seem to remember when they were little. Now I like enormously what I don't quite understand. I like grand words which make a fine sound, words that you don't use in ordinary speech. I never ask what they mean, because I prefer to ponder over them and look at them, until they make me a little frightened. And then I love books without pictures.'

. . .?

'Oh yes, godmother, you see when it says, for instance, in the story I'm reading: "There was a beautiful young girl in a castle by the side of a lake . . ." I turn the page, and I see a drawing of the castle, and the young girl, and the lake. Oh, la la!'

. . .?

'I can't explain it very well, but it never, never looks like *my* young girl, or *my* castle, or *my* lake. . . . I can't tell you why. . . . If I could paint. . . . That's why I prefer *your* books, the yellow books without pictures. . . . Do you understand me, godmother?'

. . .

'You say "yes" but I'm not sure. . . . And then, they don't talk enough about love in children's books.'

. . . !

'What've I said now? Is love a wicked word?'

. . .

'Now I don't know where I am! Me, I'm very much in love.'

. . . ?

'With no one. I realize I'm only ten and that it would be ridiculous to be in love with someone at that age. But I'm in love, just like that, nothing more. I'm waiting. That's why I'm so fond of love stories, terrible stories with a happy ending.'

. . .

'Because stories with an unhappy ending, you're upset afterwards, you can't eat, you go on thinking about it, and when you look at the cover of the book, you say to yourself: "Yes, they're going on being unhappy in there. . . ." You wonder what you can do about it, you think of writing a sequel where everything will work out. . . . I do so like it when they get married!'

. . . ?

'Yes, but after they've been very unhappy beforehand, each in their way. It's not that I hanker after these misfortunes, but it's necessary.'

. . . ?

'So there'll be a beginning, a middle and an end. And then because love, in my opinion, is to be very sad to begin with and very happy afterwards. . . .'

. . .

'No, no, not at all, it's not often just the other way round! Who asked you for your opinion? Don't bother me with your grown-up ideas! And try to write a beautiful story in your paper now, a story *for me*, not for children. A story where they cry, where they adore each other, where they get married. . . . And then put in some words I like, see, such as: *foment, surreptitious,* and *pro rata* and *corroborate* and *premonitory*. . . . And then, when you begin a new paragraph, you say: "In the meantime. . . ." '

. . .?

'I don't know exactly what it means but it looks elegant.'

My Godchild

Le Matin, 18 January, 1912

'Is that you calling, godmother? I'm here under the stairs.'

. . .?

'No, godmother, I'm not sulking.'

. . .?

'No, godmother, I'm not crying just now. I've stopped. But I'm very upset.'

. . .?

'Oh, it's always the same thing! I'm cross with Mama. And she, she's cross with me.'

. . .!

'What d'you mean, "of course"? There's absolutely no "of course" about it. There are times that she's cross with me when I don't give in – it depends whether she's fair.'

. . .!

'Oh! Please, godmother, not today! You can tell me that another day. There are plenty of days when I'm in a good mood and you can turn down my ears. . . .'[1]

. . .

'No, not *din* it into my ears[2], *turn down*! When you scold the dog, what does he do? He droops his ears. Me too, I've been drooping my ears since lunch. Now I'll start again; you can *turn down* my ears with parents, and the fair play of parents, and

---

[1] *rabattre les oreilles*
[2] *rebattre les oreilles*

how a child mustn't judge its parents, and this and that. . . .
Today, it won't work.'

. . .?

'What's the matter with me? The matter is that Mama's upset
me. Listen to what I have to say. I can talk to you best, because
you've no child. You understand me better.'

. . .!

'Yes, it is logical. You've no child, you've still got a mother,
you get told off, you rave, you rage, and then you have the
reputation of not being reasonable; Mama shrugs her shoulders
when she talk about you, the same as with me. . . . I like that.
It gives me confidence.'

. . .

'Please don't mention it, I don't do it on purpose. . . . Now
then, I'm going to get nearer the fire: I'd had enough of that,
under the stairs, you know! There then. Mama upsets me. I can't
get her to understand certain things.'

. . .?

'Serious things, things about life. Imagine, she's just bought
me a hat to go to school with! . . . Oh yes, it's true, you wouldn't
know, you're not from these parts. . . . At Montigny the lay
school pupils *never* wear a hat, except in summer for the sun,
and even, I tell you this under the sound of secrecy . . .'

. . .!

'The *sound*, I tell you! The proof is that it means one is
speaking in a low voice, eh! . . . Well then, I tell you under the
sound of secrecy that we boo the pupils of the Sisters in the street
because they don't go to school bareheaded. You won't tell
anyone?'

. . .!

'Good. Well then, Mama's bought me a hat. I looked pretty
glum at that hat! Naturally, Mama begins a two hour speech
which has nothing to do with the matter: how I'm gone ten, and
I'm almost a young girl, and I must set an example of faultless
get-up . . . In the end, she really got me down. I lost my temper,
I told her it was no affair of hers, that my school life was a
private life which parents don't understand, eccetera . . . "Look,
Mama," I said to her, "do you get involved in telling Papa what
he has to do in his office? When I'm at school, it's the same thing.

I'm in a very conspicuous position at school, a very delicate situation, because I've a personality, so Mademoiselle says. To listen to you, Mama, I should only think about the family! You send me to school, I spend half my life there : well then, that counts, half my life. . . . School is like another world, they speak differently there : what's all right here won't do at school, and if I tell you that I mustn't go to class with a hat in winter, it's because I mustn't wear a hat! In fact, Mama, these are things one just knows, they're nuances!" I reeled all this off to her very calmly, all at one go, so that she shouldn't have time to put in a word, because you know what mamas are like, don't you? They get carried away, they get carried away, and then they lose their sense of proportion . . .'

. . .?

'I mean that they're all fire and fury, just as much over a broken glass as for something very, very wicked. Especially mine. She is impressionable. Afterwards, she looked at me as if I'd fallen from the moon and said very quietly : "My God, this child . . . this child!" She looked so miserable and astonished, you'd have thought it was me who'd been scolding her. So much so that I seized her like this, by the neck, and cuddled her against me like this, saying : "There, there, my little darling, there! . . ." It all ended very well.'

. . .?

'But yes! We're fed up with each other, but for another reason. The business of the hat, that was yesterday. Today . . . see, look at my finger.'

. . .!

'Yes, a cut, a deep one, and the nail's split. It's had hydrogen peroxide and I don't know what on it. And here, on my cheek, you can see a red burn; that smarts. And my hair, do you notice anything, on my forehead? Feel it : it must feel a bit like when they singe the pig in the square. All these are today's troubles, which have upset both of us, Mama and me. . . . I wanted a curled fringe on my forehead; so I cut a few locks – but that's nothing! I'm well aware that one always goes farther with scissors than one wishes. . . . And I burnt my cheek trying to twist the iron to make it colder, you know, like the hairdresser; it makes it so pretty. . . .

. . .?

'The cut, that's the scissors. A little more, and I'd have put my eye out. . . . So you can see me, can't you, with my hand full of blood, my hair scorched and cut all zig-zag, my cheek burnt. . . . And of course, Mama had to come home at that very moment! What I had to put up with, my dear!'

. . .!

'Yes, I was in the wrong, but she scolded me far beyond the ordinary. I assure you, it wasn't a matter of the proprieties any more, or of dress, or of children who touch everything and get punished for it! It wasn't even a question of me, hardly!'

. . .?

'Wait, let me remember. . . . She was like a fury. She said that I had ruined *her* child! She said: "What have you done with *my* beautiful hair which I cherish so patiently? You'd no right to touch it! And that cheek, who gave you permission to injure it? And this little hand? . . . Well? . . . I can devote years, I can pass days and nights trembling over this masterpiece, and it takes just one of your actions, you destructive little devil, to spoil the adorable produce of so much care! It's dastardly, it's shameful, what you've done there! Your beauty belongs to me, you haven't the right to diminish a trust that I confide to you!" What d'you think of that, godmother?'

. . .

'Me neither, I couldn't think of anything to say. But it came to me. I went under the stairs without breathing a word. And I punished myself as much as possible. I felt my hands, my legs, my head: "My poor darling," I said to myself, "your hands, your legs, your head don't even belong to you! You're just like a slave! . . . A lot of good it's done you, your mother giving you birth, if she takes back everything else! You mustn't ever dare to lose a milk tooth or break a nail, in case your mother asks you for it back. . . ." In fact, you know, how one talks to oneself when one wants to make oneself cry. . . . Ah! I've a mother who causes me plenty of suffering, godmother.'

. . .

'You think I get my own back! It's possible. And then, if she's kind to me at table, perhaps I can forgive her?'

. . .

'I do want to. It's true, she called me a destructive devil,
but . . .'

. . .?

'But she also called me an "adorable product" and that's nice,
after all.'

A Hairdresser

Le Matin, 20 January, 1914

'We shan't be disturbed here, Madame, in this small back salon.
Shampoo?'

. . .

'Oh, I know how it goes! You haven't the time, just an
antiseptic! And then afterwards, you complain about having
matted hair. I'll wager you're going to the dress-rehearsal at the
Gymnase? I knew it! How did you like the one at the Ambigu?'

. . .

'It didn't come up to my expectations. Nothing really new,
nothing startling, no bright ideas. Not one entrance to bring out
the cry.'

. . .?

'The cry, you know, the cry: "Now *there's* a good one!" '

. . .?

'Why, a coiffure, of course! There, as everywhere, it was a
mish-mash of ideas; yes, that's the expression I was searching
for! You could see the badly-combed, the sugar-loaf, the kiss-
curl, the eternal turban, the tulle fly-bag enveloping the head.
. . . Mind your eyes with this spirit vapour. . . . Next time, I'll
make you a fine shampoo with raw eggs.'

. . .?

'Is it good? It's excellent . . . for the egg marketers. Ah! Ah!'

. . .!

'Sorry, the comb got caught up. You've got scurf.'

. . .!

'No, I was mistaken. Take no notice; it was just that we'd reached the point where I always say that . . . to ordinary clients. But me, I'm so unbusinesslike! You see, I don't insist. We are old acquaintances.'

. . .

'Not at all, the pleasure is mine. Anyway, I haven't a shred of malice, I leave to a certain colleague the trick about falling hair from lying-in.'

. . .?

'You don't know it? It's simple. A client – I mean a lady – loses her hair at the temples and the edge of the forehead after having had a baby, it's inevitable, but it grows again six months later. What does my colleague do? He says: "You're losing your hair here, there, and here too." . . . "Oh, my God!" says the lady . . . "Don't worry," puts in the coiffeur, "we have a toilet water here which . . . a water that. . . ." To cut it short, three months later the lady sees her hair sprouting again and sings like anything the praises of the water which . . . of the water that . . . Shall I give you a wave?'

. . .?

'It's a matter of a quarter of an hour. Honestly, you ask me that every time. And every time I answer: "It's a matter of a quarter of an hour" as is proper for any procedure that takes twenty-five minutes. What dress are you wearing tonight?'

. . .

'Yes, yes, I know it, gold lamé on a night-blue background. You haven't looked at all bad in it before.'

. . .!

'Certainly not, I've no intention of offering you another. Even if my means permitted such fancies, my clientele would certainly not allow it. Ah! ah! . . . But we could rejuvenate your blue dress.'

. . .?

'With a pretty wig of the same shade.'

. . .!

'Jump up and down if you like, but not too high because I've got hold of the hair on your neck. A pretty little blue wig, I said.

With two rows of small imitation jewels and a rocket-shower of blue bird-of-paradise feathers. . . . It's good, it's good, you'll come round to it!'

. . .!

'Maybe not *you* personally, but your best friend, your tea-party acquaintances, your sister-in-law, your cousin, in fact, those to whom you say, speaking of coloured hair: "How horrible! If ever I see you with dead apple-green hair on your head, I'll pick a quarrel with you!" Well, they'll wear it, they're wearing it already, and you don't pick a quarrel with them. And I, I your coiffeur, I laugh in my little corner.'

. . .

'No, not because of that. It's because I tell myself that I, coiffeur, simple *merlan*¹ that I am, nevertheless have more influence over your personal friends than you have yourself. It really doubles me up. I've nearly finished.'

. . .!

'Yes, I still say it's pretty. You know, a beautiful violet or night-blue wig such as I suggest is ravishing for the complexion. It's good for you, it creates contrasts.'

. . .?

'Do I know what a contrast is? Of course I know. A contrast, that's . . . er . . . there, like that . . . something blurred . . . that's got it!'

. . .?

'Now a white wig, that's not so satisfactory. It has a fascination, sometimes, for very young women and for old ladies who dye. Because the old ladies who dye tell themselves: "The day I don't want to dye any more, I shall have my hair quite white, like a young woman!"'

. . .?

'No, they go on dyeing. The idea was enough for them. We've finished, a little brilliantine?'

. . .?

'It gives a sheen. It gives an extraordinary sheen . . . to the lining of hats. Ah! ah! Just glance in the workshop before you

---

¹ A *merlan* is a fish. When hairdressers were mainly occupied with preparing and powdering wigs, they became so powdered themselves that they were teased with resembling floured *merlans* waiting to be fried.

leave, I've a small selection of wigs in colours you've never seen.
. . . Eh, what did you say?'

. . .!

'No, you won't see them in Paris. Do you know where they go?
To Germany. I've had orders for thirty at a time from Berlin.
Made in France! *Pariser kunst*! Why, I've sent them cabbage-
green and casserole yellow and soft pink, and that one over there,
look, Parma mauve, and Prussian blue, naturally. . . . And I
charge them for those six, seven, eight hundred smackers apiece,
oh my word! One is a patriot in one's own way: it's still the
same amount of money coming in.'

A Masseuse

Le Matin, 5 February, 1914

'Pouh! . . . Good-day, Madame. Pouh! my word, I'm tired!
And how's the knee?'

. . .

'So you say, so you say. Let's have a look. It's true the swell-
ing's going down. But the place is still pretty black with extrava-
sated blood. It was a really bad knock, that. My word, I'm
tired!'

. . .?

'Why don't I sit down then? Ah, yes. . . . Take no notice, I
say that every now and then, that I'm tired. I say it because it's
the truth: I can't hold up any more, I give way. It's a real
pleasure.'

. . .?

'Just think, Madame, it's killing here. All these ladies are like
madwomen. One wants to go off to the Midi, another's just back
from there, another never stops going out at night, and all those
who are exhausted from dancing the tango – and the worst of all
are those who don't dance, don't go out and don't travel – those

are the ones who wear out my doormat most. . . . All of them,
I tell you! . . . It's got to the point that when I get to you, a
week now since your sprain, I exclaim : "Ah, my God, now for
half an hour's rest, a peaceful little sitting down massage!" The
leg more relaxed, absolutely limp, if you please.'

  . . .?

'Don't be a tease! From that to saying you did well to sprain
your knee, that's a great difference! But anyway, I'm very happy
to take you between two big massages. When I leave you, I go
. . . a long way away, at the far end of Auteuil.'

  . . .?

'You know very well that I never say to whom. To the lady
I've told you about, who is so rich and so bad-tempered : you
know well enough. She receives me like a dog if I'm two minutes
late, especially now when she's without a first parlourmaid; she
engaged one, a pearl, who stayed in the house an hour . . . it's
enough to make you die laughing! The parlourmaid arrives, a
very nice girl; the lady, who'd lunched well, exclaims on seeing
her : "But she's very nice! A really roguish little soubrette!
You're going to be called Marton, and we'll be on familiar
terms!" To which the parlourmaid retorts : "I don't mind about
the name; but, as to the familiarity, if Madame doesn't mind, in
my opinion we really haven't known each other long enough,
Madame and I."'

  . . .

'Sure, that wasn't badly spoken. Only, it cost her her place.
To be so witty at a hundred and twenty francs a month, at that
rate I'd rather be an animal. Pouh, I'm tired!'

  . . .

'I should rest? You can't mean it! First, I don't like it. I'm
made to work first and complain afterwards. If I don't complain,
I'm not happy. Look, days like tomorrow : at five o'clock in the
morning, my Greek lady . . .'

  . . .?

'I mean it : five o'clock in the morning. Ah, if you're looking
for a cushy billet, I don't advise you to get a job as a domestic
with her. She doesn't sleep and it irritates her that others do. At
five in the morning she's hanging on all the bell-pulls, waiting for
the staff to come down, she runs in her kimono to hide little balls

of paper behind or under all the furniture to see if they'll be
swept up. Even me she stops from sleeping. It's out of pure malice
that she wants her body massage at five; she'd pay me anything,
just for the pleasure of asking me when I arrive : "Well, my poor
Antoinette, it can't have been very warm coming this morning.
My thermometer shows six below, behind the window!" Then I
swank a bit; I answer : "A little chilly, Madame, a little chilly. It
makes the blood tingle. If you walked around in the street at this
hour, you wouldn't have butter-coloured legs as you do have,
probably." '

. . .

'Well, I can be spiteful too. Last winter, she very nearly
arranged for me at eight in the morning, but she changed her
mind. She must have considered that the Metro is running at that
hour, and the buses, and that would have made things too easy
for me. She's got a glib tongue, my word! She knows French as
well as a cab-driver. I used to go red in the face, sometimes, the
insults she'd give me. Once I took my courage in both hands and
said to her : "Madame, tomorrow it will be fifty francs instead
of forty." "And may I ask why?" she replies. "Two louis for the
massage and ten francs for the swear-words." '

. . .

'How well you behave when you're kept amused! You're as
still as my big daddy, as I call him, my retired colonel, when I
massage his poor wrists. He comes next after my Greek lady. And
so it goes on from hour to hour all the rest of the day, until eight
in the evening. And just think, if one of my clients cancels, I feel
the ground giving way under my feet, I see myself ruined and
destroyed, can you imagine? In the evening I finish with my
English lady, and when I get there, I massage her in a kind of
trance, I'm so worn out with exhaustion! A pretty blonde lady,
my English lady, well-made and all. But she's got a bee in her
bonnet, too.'

. . .?

'She belongs to a special religion and she wants me to join
too . . . "Antoinette," she says, "you've got to be a Christian
Scientist." "That sounds very difficult, the very sound of the
name," I reply. "On the contrary," says my lady, "it's a religion
which guarantees perfect happiness to all its adopts , , , adepts.

Look, you who are always tired, repeat firmly : *I am not tired,*
and by applying your thoughts strongly enough to convince yourself of it, you'll be able to suppress the feeling of fatigue entirely.
Again, when you're unhappy . . ." – "Yes, Madame! yes,
Madame" I interrupt, "I understand, I'll try it." Why should
I set out to contradict a good client? . . . Last night I arrive at
my English lady's and I find her all anyhow. "Oh, Antoinette,"
she tells me, "my clip, my beautiful clip with two large diamonds
and a grey pearl, I've lost it! You can't think how upset I am."
– "Well, Madame," I reply, "now or never's the time to repeat
to yourself firmly : '*I have not lost my clip, I have not lost my
clip, I have not lost my clip!* . . .' " '

. . . ?

'She didn't say anything, but she gave me a nasty look. Pouh!
. . . We've finished while we've been chatting. You feel it tingling,
don't you? That's how it should be! And now I'm off. . . . My
bag, what have I done with my bag? Oh dear, my God, my bag,
the iodized cream's in it! There's a client who's waiting for my
iodized cream like the Messiah! . . . My bag, my iodized cream,
my keys, my purse, my . . . Ah, there it is! Pouh! That's better.'

. . .

'No, not your knee, me! Goodnight, Madame, I must rush. . . .'

My Corset-Maker

Fantasio, p. 321–322

Characters: My corset-maker, a stout lady, asthmatic, who looks as if she never wore corsets. Me, sullen and rebellious.

The scene represents a very small salon. Photographs on the mantelpiece, signed. A chromolithograph on the wall, portraying a vagely female larva of worm-like thinness, with this legend: "The corset PERI 327 allows both the seated and the standing positions."

MY CORSET-MAKER: 'Ah! Good-day, Madame. I'd given up hope of seeing you this season! I said to myself: "Is it possible that she's going behind my back?"'

. . .

'Yes, I do know that you travel a lot. Travel, that's fatal to the waistline. You buy corsets here and there, even in the fancy goods shops, and that's how you get deformed! You come at a bad time; with all these ladies going away for the summer, I don't know which way to turn.'

. . .

'Oh! But you've put on weight since last year!'

. . .

'You certainly have put on weight! Look here . . . and here. . . . How could you have let yourself get like that? And with fashions what they are, what can you have been thinking of?'

. . .

'Oh, I'm not happy about you, not happy at all! . . . Anyway, undress: I've got a pattern of my new model, my 327, ready for you. . . .'

. . .

'Of course, of course it will suit you. . . . And what's all this? You're wearing only two suspenders now!'

145

. . .

'Maybe it is more convenient! But I wonder what you would
do if you were like many of these ladies with a fat lower stomach.
A fat lower stomach, that isn't conjured away like a hundred-
sou coin.'

. . .

'Oh! What are you saying! Ah, you're all the same, you'll
make me blush. . . . It's like those ladies who make themselves
thin; it's necessary for the *mode*, isn't it? They listened to me,
they got thin; only, they've too much skin, right? They've too
much skin on the abdomen especially, and then under the arms,
too, at the level of the breasts. . . . It's a job, a job for a real
artist, arranging that and putting everything in order. Madame X,
you know her, that fine woman with a sable coat worth two
hundred and twenty-five thousand? She's a new client. She is
superb, you wouldn't recognize her any more. What a waist!
What hips! Like this, see. And she was so strong! Well, she has
too much skin, that's understandable. But with my 327, she's
divine!'

. . .?

'And when she undresses? Oh, my word, that's her affair.
Who hasn't been in that position, the way things are nowadays?'

. . .

'What d'you mean, that's idiotic? I could quote you fifty.
I could quote you a hundred, who are no more idiotic than you
or I! You come here with your other-wordly ideas, but you won't
change anything, in spite of your little belts which thicken your
silhouette and make you lopsided! I've had clients who started
by wanting to react against the fashion, as you do, they end up
like the others! They can't win. . . . Strange! You've no varicose
veins?'

. . .

'That's funny. I've never seen so many as this year.'

. . .

'Do you imagine that's our fault? Varicose veins come by
themselves. I don't say as much for that poor Madame Z. Do
you know her? She's smothered in varicose veins. Veins like

irrigation pipes! You won't tell anyone? My word, how fat you've got!'

. . .

'No, it's not just my idea! You don't make an effort, you calmly accept it . . . Ah! You're not an energetic woman like Madame P . . .'

. . .?

'What does she do? She *drives* the fat away. At first she had rather thick hips: "Madame Adèle," she says to me, "I don't want my hips any more! See to it!" So I lengthen her corsets liberally and I pull them together below, ha! . . . The fat shifts gradually and moves down to the thigh. But on the thigh it makes a roll. I lengthen the corsets again generously, I gather together, ha. . . . So well that Madame P ends up by having her rolls of fat right down below where they are scarcely visible. She is delighted. It's the same with the bosom.'

. . .?

'No one wants the bosom any more. The princess dress, the flat sheath, all these have dethroned the bosom. These ladies have done everything they could: they have *distributed* it to left and right, they have expelled it to some extent under the arms. But what's uglier than a fold of flesh at the armpit? We can do better than that nowadays!'

. . .?

'Well then, we take hold of the breast like this. . . . Don't be afraid! I'll explain it to you with a piece of material. . . . We catch the breast, see, like this, and we double it over downwards, folding it as close as possible against the ribs. On top you fix a little brassiere: my 14b, a gem! It's not properly speaking a *soutien-gorge*, it's a little elastic tissue to keep the breast in position. And, on top of everything, you put on my corset, my great 327, the marvel of the day. And there you are with a divine outline, no more hip, or belly, or backside than a bottle of Rhine wine, and above all the chest of an ephebe. To have the chest of an ephebe, that's something. It had to come! Ah well, Madame, I have competitors who've invented this and that. The tissue vest, the elastic band to bring together and compress both halves of the backside, the tape between the legs, but I can say that I have been the first to render practicable, and truly aesthetic, the management of the "folded breast"!'

The Saleslady

21 May, 1914

At the milliner's. A client arrives, the saleslady comes running: twenty-five years old, the eyes of a young tyrant, a turret of blonde hair on top of her head. Hands, waist, mouth, feet, all are slender to excess, witty and aggressive.

'Ah! At last, Madame! you've come back to us! I was beginning to despair. I said to myself: "That's it! She'll have gone to Harry's to have some Berlin-style hats made!" But what *have* you got on your head then?'

. . .?

'Yes, the thing with a blue wing at the side and velvet all round?'

. . .?

'What, you made it yourself? All by yourself. But it's unbelievable, it's miraculous! If I may allow myself a joke, you've a future in fashion. Would you honour our house by joining it as a finisher?'

. . .?

'A finisher? She's . . . my goodness, she's the one who fixes the linings inside the hats, who . . . well . . . who does a lot of little things. Let me have it, your darling "creation", oh, I'll give it back to you! Look, I'll return it . . . let's see . . . tomorrow. That's it, tomorrow. Actually, the car delivers in your suburb tomorrow.'

. . .?

'Yes, of course, I meant to say your district. It's so far away!
I'm only a poor Parisian with never the time to leave my place,
you see. The boulevard in winter, Deauville in summer, the
Biarritz branch in September, Monte-Carlo in January. . . . Ah,
we can't all live in Auteuil. . . . Come with me, quickly, I've a
nice corner in the small salon looking into the street. It's badly
lit? You don't like having your back to the light? But it's the best
place for trying on hats, you know! The silhouette's outlined
against the window, and this season it's the silhouette that matters
most of all; no one's paying any attention to details. And then,
see, you're between Mademoiselle X, the singer, who's just trying
on hats for her tour, and Princess Z who's arrived from the
south.'

. . .

'Yes, that one, that fat old lady. In the business we call her
the Fairy-Rose.'

. . .?

'Because, whenever a hat doesn't suit her, she always says: "I
think it lacks something, there, in the hollow . . . some trifle, a little
flower . . . a bunch of fairy-roses!" Mademoiselle X, there she is,
on your left, she isn't exactly pretty, but she's so good-hearted!'

. . .?

'Oh, a heart of gold. . . . Look, the lady who's with her, yes,
that kind of little shark in black, that's a poor friend she's picked
up. She takes her everywhere with her, to her couturier's, to her
jeweller's; – here, she spends hours trying on twenty-five hats
under her poor friend's nose – to amuse her.

'Now, suppose we talk seriously for a moment. I've taken it
into my head to ruin you today. It was on a day like this that
I went into business. Now, to start with, stick this little cap on
your beautiful hair! . . . Haven't you changed its colour?'

. . .

'It's the bad light. I said to myself: it's more golden than
usual. You might have thought about changing it just for the
sake of changing. . . . And then, some people go white very early.
. . . On the side, on the side, completely covering one ear! There!
How do you find it?'

. . . !

'I can see it's not a success. In any case, you're right, it's not your type of hat. On you, it looks a little . . . a little ladylike. It's funny, I've just sold the same thing to Mrs W. . . . She looks ravishing in it, Mrs W . . . she's got a long slender neck and, on top of that, a chin, such fresh cheeks, and ears. . . . For the moment let's give this model up for lost; for every one lost we'll find ten more. . . . Look, what was I saying! Here's the very thing. You've pulled it well down, haven't you?'

. . .

'More than that, more than that! I can still see the hair on your forehead, and where it grows out at the back! I expect you know the "great hat principle of the season", as the *patronne* calls it?'

. . . ?

'The great principle is that when you meet a woman in the street, and her hat lets you know whether she is dark, fair or chestnut, then the lady in question isn't wearing a smart hat. There! . . . Notice that I'm saying nothing, I'm leaving you to make up your own mind. Well?'

. . .

'Do you prefer the navy blue? The one that's there, on the stand? Yes? . . . That's right then! . . .'

. . .

'No, no, it's not sold.'

. . .

'Not at all, Madame, I don't want to stop you from buying it! I didn't suggest it to you, because. . . . I didn't know I had enough talent to sell hats like that to you. But it's true that it suits your face! Ah! you know what you want, you do! As I always say, there are only two classes of client whose ideas you can't change : artists and small shopkeepers.'

. . .

'You're no artist, but all the same you've a very independent judgement. Try this one on, to please me. There's nothing exaggerated about it, but to my mind it's both rich and discreet, because of that fancy notion in oil cloth which gives it style. . . . No? Ah! I'm out of luck, you only want to hurt my feelings. . . . If your two sons are like you in character, they'll be terrible men!

Are they well, those two great babies?'

. . .

'Already? My goodness, how time passes! And still handsome
I'm sure. Not that it's anything to be surprised at.'

. . .!

'No, Madame, there's no flattery intended; besides, everyone
in the establishment is of the same opinion, they all say the same
about your husband's presence, charm and intelligence . . . and
it's well known that your two loves of children have also inherited
your fine health! What a pity they aren't girls! I'd be doing
their hats already and I'd spoil them as much as you do. . . . Well
then, for today, just the little blue hat? Shall I have it sent down
to the car?'

. . .

'Yes, yes, don't be afraid. I'll give the description of the car
to the page-boy myself. Do you think I don't know it, the dark
brown landaulet, you've had it six years! Goodbye, Madame,
and thank you for your kind visit, don't leave it so long before
coming to see your faithful saleslady; – I so much enjoy seeing
you. . . . It's a rest after our American clients: as for them, I
only want to tell them unpleasant things!'

An Interview

Le Matin, 25 June, 1914

'Yes, dear lady, it's me! Confound destiny, it's me again! You haven't forgotten our last interview? How you ill-treated me! I can see you still, at the end of our discussion, in those extraordinary corridors of the People's University. . . . "What has he come here for?" you grumbled between your teeth. . . . Yes, yes, don't deny it, I heard you clearly! The fact is that my evening dress was singularly out of place in that working-class environment. . . .'

. . .

'You're right, it's not a working-class environment, it's an environment . . . prompt me with the expression . . . of the people! There: an environment of the people! And now, let us talk seriously. This time I take the seat that you don't offer me and I settle down – what am I saying? I dig myself in! Our old camaraderie grants me rights, and no one shall have, before I do, the little piece about your new book. . . . Understand me, I'd like something a little different from the eternal: "We found the highly original artist at her work-desk, between her police dog and her Siamese cat . . ." Between you and me, we've seen enough of your animals! I want to present to our readers a real "you", a "you" that has been explored somewhat, a "you" in depth, a little . . . Observe that I've got a pencil and notebook! I very much enjoy playing the reporter who notes down run-over dogs and holes in the boulevards. It's so unlike me to act the little journalist. . . .'

. . .

'Yes, yes, the little journalist, I like this expression, its despondency expresses adequately the sadness, pettiness and emptiness of a profession which is no profession. . . . That surprises you, admit it, to hear me say such melancholy things. . . . It's because I've just gone through, and I'm only just through it, a rotten time.'

. . .?

'Oh! . . . everything and nothing . . . Neurasthenia. A vague word which contains so many exact miseries. . . . It's got to the stage when I'm still asking myself: well, shall I take myself to the country, with the few pennies my father left me, to plant cabbages, live obscurely and . . . how shall I put it? Monastically . . . That would be wise perhaps . . . And so much the worse for the blackened sheets of paper, the useless offspring of my thoughts! . . .'

. . .?

'Yes . . . I have on the stocks . . . how shall I describe it? . . . a study, a vast "study of man" – I'm fond of this title, which is reminiscent of Balzac's *Etudes de femmes* . . . I'm going to talk to you with the frankness of a colleague: my book once finished – isn't it? At each moment I lean over my hero as if over an abyss, and I cry: "But I didn't know him! – But I'm only half-seeing him!" It's this exhausting task which has brought me where I am: neurasthenia, insomnia, uncertain appetite, migraines, etc. And the job, all this time, the terrible job which won't wait, which asserts itself, which drives you on: go on, the queen of the Sainte-Marguerite market is calling you, the playwright whose play's going on tomorrow is awaiting you! Then the over-tired body revolts, the nerves get out of hand, one comes down in full flight! . . . You know all that, you've suffered all that, of course. . . .'

. . .

'Go on, go on, it's not worth denying it, we're talking heart to heart, listening to you it seems to me that your soul reflects mine a little, I'm so happy, so honoured by this similarity of impressions! What did you do to overcome the crisis?'

. . .

'. . . In my case, I was first affected by . . . how shall I put it? . . . a phobia for noise and light, I went so far as to experience the infantilism of lining my shutters, of lining my walls with cork. . . . I've even gone so far – it's enough to make you laugh out of pity! – as to offer to buy a carpet for my neighbours upstairs. . . . I lived like a prisoner, lit by a solitary lamp: anaemia – I stop the word on your lips – was not long in coming;

then there began the tedious treatments destined to invigorate a
wretched organism that was young yet exhausted.

'I've experienced cold water therapy, raw horse-meat, the spa
– oh, what a book, if I had had the strength, in that season at
the spa – and for results that were illusory, purely illusory. . . .
What do you think I did then?'

. . .

'Yes, yes, you see what's coming! I said to myself: You will
forget your trouble in taking an interest in the suffering of others,
you will see yourself humbly in their small-mindedness, in their
ambitions, you will confess to what they conceal; in a word : you
will be a reporter! But a reporter rather as one is a doctor, or
a detective; you will not mingle with the crowd of those who
limit themselves to the role of dictaphone and camera, no! From
an imprudent word you will construct an anecdote; from a smile
or a gesture, you will make a short novel. . . . A novel as tranquil,
certainly, as the one that shelters between the walls and beneath
the foliage of this garden. . . . Isn't that so? . . . Ah! it's delightful. . . . This provincial corner, this lime-scented air. . . . That's
what my wretched nerves could have done with, but . . . without
being indiscreet, how much is your rent? . . .'

. . .

'Well, well! . . . Paradise is worth paying for. . . . A paradise
without heating? . . . No? with heating? Fine. And do you think
that round here I might find . . .

. . .

'Oh! that's what you say. . . . You would really like to attract
your colleague and friend down here? All the same, we could
arrange a charming set-up in a maisonnette like this, only with
horrible Restoration furniture . . . combined washstands and
dressing-tables, undersized washbasins in flowered porcelain. . . .
I've a genius for furnishing, you know. . . . Oh! I shan't think
any more about it! It's certainly your fault, you'll have to pay
for it!'

. . .

'Ah! ah! . . . Who's going to find herself in *L'Heure* tomorrow, depicted from head to foot, with her femininity and
hyperaesthetic sensitivity? It's you, my dear friend, it's you!'

. . .

'What, you haven't opened your mouth? Ah! just like a woman, that remark, just like a woman! In that remark alone there are a hundred lines about psychology! . . . Don't women live entirely in their silence? I must go or you'll scratch my eyes out, for a woman will forgive a man – even a reporter – everything, except perspicacity. And I shall steal one of your roses – I've a passion for flowers! If I had not been today entirely the slave of my profession – and of a curiosity compounded of liking and admiration – I should have described to you how I arrived at this flower-cult, that's the strangest thing of all. . . But today, facts first! Dear Madame and friend, the little journalist kisses your hands and rushes to his factory – but the friend remains pensively at your feet, on this lawn they barely touch. . . .